HOW YOU LEAVE THEM FEELING

Your Ultimate Key to Personal & Professional Success

JESSE FERRELL

Publisher: JessTalk Speaking Services, LLC

Senior Project Consultant: Rob Ciccone, President - Success Unlimited

Editor: Patricia Anderson, PhD Literary Consultant

Contributing Editors: Ann Lee, President - Ann Lee & Associates
                      Cher Weldon, Partner - Ann Lee & Associates

Creative Director: Timothy Tweed - Success Unlimited

Jacket design and copy: Success Unlimited Sales & Marketing Group (www.susmg.com)

Photography: Michael Markovic

Printed in Canada

Library of Congress Catalogue Number:
ISBN-10: 0-9778810-0-8
ISBN-13: 978-0-9778810-0-0

Ferrell, Jesse
1. Self-help   2. Self-improvement

Table of Contents

Foreword
By Louis Gossett, Jr.
Academy Award® Winner
"An Officer and a Gentleman" (1982)

It is a foregone conclusion that all uplifting books like this have no use if we are not open, ready, willing, and prepared to take the words off the page and practice them in our daily lives. You must be ready to improve the quality of your life, no matter what you read, or no book is going to work for you. That is why there are Phi Beta Kappa people on skid row. In order to grow, we must all be prepared to take the wisdom from books like this and apply it to our lives to the fullest extent. If you approach this book enthusiastically and are determined to improve the quality of your life, watch it happen one page at a time... it's a guarantee!

I have done it in my life and this book has helped me invaluably! Every day I can see its results. The points in this book are all steps in a ladder; each level takes care of a different part of the self: psyche, spirit, health, education, attitude, and actions. And all of this leads toward the same conclusion: By taking the words off the pages of "How You Leave Them Feeling", and by applying them, along with the tools provided for taking full measure of where you are in your life, you will see positive results on a daily basis.

For all of us, problems still exist, but the quality of the problems may be much higher than they were before. One thing has to do with paying the rent and another has to do with how you go to the next level in your business. Before reading this book, you may have problems such as "I need to buy a new pair of shoes," or "I need to buy another battery for the car," or "Do I have enough gas to get from here to there?" Afterward, before you know it, you are thinking: "Can I get a new car? Is my house good enough? What about insurance for my children or employees?" The next thing you know, you find yourself thinking about things such as "Should I buy this building, or is this airplane good enough for my crew?" The fact is, you will always have to manage problems, but the quality of the problems can get higher and higher. Think of it this way: A low-quality problem may be buying a toothbrush and a high-quality problem may be buying a factory.

In solving your problems, you will need help along the way, and we must all agree to that. The global community is the ultimate salvation of the world; the global community is the only way to go. You can't give away what you don't have, and therefore, from books like this, you must learn how to add yourself to the global community. Otherwise, you have nothing to give to the global community and you become a detriment to it.

The best way to contribute to the global community is by self-improvement -by going to the next level and living up to your potential in life. Once there, you must add your efforts and achievements to the melting pot of the global community - this helps to get rid of racism, jealousy, rage, and anger. In motivating people to improve and succeed, books like this one are the ultimate foundation for the betterment of the human race.

Louis Gossett, Jr.

Preface

The fact that you are now reading these words is a testimony to how people find a way to accomplish the important things in life. I wrote this book to help deliver a very simple message for anyone seeking to live the life they desire. There are seven essential laws of life, and together they reveal the awesome power and truth of the concept of "How You Leave Them Feeling". The goal is to leave everyone that you encounter feeling good about themselves and about you.

I have written this book over hundreds of hours as I traveled literally tens of thousands of miles to faraway places. There was the time from Las Vegas to Toronto, Canada, when I wrote on the airplane. There was the time when I sat in the airport in Puerto Plata, Dominican Republic, awaiting my return flight home to Las Vegas. I found peace of mind in writing this book during an entire flight from Newark, New Jersey, to Paris, France.

Writing about the Law of Personal and Professional Development gave me solace during the train ride across breathtaking countryside villages from Paris to Geneva, Switzerland. The journey from Geneva to Cannes and St. Tropez, in the south of France, brought with it new inspirations. Later, as I sat atop a peak overlooking the serene and expansive Mediterranean Sea at St. Tropez, it seemed only fitting that I would experience an epiphany while writing the laws of accumulation and attraction.

As I traveled to Naples and Rome, Italy, with my very good friend and client, Derek Elliott, our twice-daily runs through the Villa Borghese Park brought clarity and focus. The walls of the Roman Colosseum echoed my belief in the Law of Accumulation and set the tone for the chapter on that topic.

The small town of Orangeville and the big-city appeal of Toronto created dramatic opposing backdrops to launch the chapter about friends, family, and the global community in which we all live. As I returned to the U.S. and covered the territories of Houston, Texas, and Los Angeles, California, I was writing the chapter on the Law of Balance and the section called "A World of Appreciation"; appropriately enough, I completed this just as my schedule took me home again to Las Vegas, Nevada. I trust you will enjoy this book and the journey through the paradigm of how you leave them feeling.

My deepest, most sincere thanks are reserved for the love of my life, my wife Teresa Ferrell, who has always been the pillar of support throughout my educational and professional pursuits. This book is hereby dedicated to her and to all she has given me. We have enjoyed a wonderful 20-plus years together on our journey thus far, and we are just getting to the good part of life together! We have learned to live our best lives now.

This book could not have been written without help from my supreme support system, starting with God. A very special thank you must also go out to my "Mastermind Coalition" of personal and professional role models and mentors: Derek F.C. Elliott, Louis Gossett, Jr., Frederick C. Elliott, John Bradley, Jason Burley, Brian Tracy, Charles Meeks, Norma Meeks, Whoopi Goldberg, Ann Lee, Pam Ferrell, Robert Ciccone, Vittorio Ciccone, Palma Ciccone, Larry Lewin, Cher Weldon, Lisa Bybee, Joe Kichler, Betty Elliott-Kichler, Darryl Odom, Jasmine Odom, Gary Selesner, Shelley Banner, Damencele DiPasqua Gradyan, Eric Zilewicz, Horst D. Zuira, Sheri Disney, Roy Disney, Bruce Davis, Donna Ludwig Peterson, Sandie Essenpreis, Daryl Tomlinson, Nancy Raphael, Jim Kilby, Letha Benjamin, Helen Harrison, George Harrison, Willie Mae Ferrell, and Jesse Ferrell Sr. These superstars gave me faith, trust and encouragement, and they always lifted my spirit when the world had taken my energy. As a result of personal and professional coaching, I was constantly being told what I could do, rather than what I couldn't do. My path as an author, lifestyle coach and professional speaker has been carved from the stone of strength that I continue to receive from this group.

We have heard it said many times that it takes a village to raise a child. Well, in my case, it has taken an international cast of villagers in my global community to shine the light on my journey to success. Each and every one has played a big role in strengthening my voice!

Jesse Ferrell
October 2005

Introduction

This book will help you navigate through the mine fields of life with maximum ease, cooperation and good fortune, while living what I call "the good life now." You have the power within you to make the difference, to turn the tide, or to tip the scales in your favor - if you only believed and understood that power. If you could tap into resources both natural and contrived, you could be effortlessly enriched by getting what you want out of life. This book will challenge you to live the life you deserve, through the observance of one key factor: how you leave others feeling.

I wrote this book to help those who feel involuntarily isolated or who lack the assistance they need from others. Do you feel like you always get the smallest steak at the dinner table of life? The chapters that follow may be your key to unlocking the secrets of getting that 28-ounce porterhouse steak with all the trimmings and plenty of leftovers to feast on for another day.

There is an old adage that has been used by Zig Ziglar and many other powerful inspirational speakers: "If you help enough people get what they want, they will ultimately help you to get what you want." While this pearl of wisdom is certainly true, we are generally not told how to do this. The best place to begin helping others get what they want is to be secure within yourself, knowing who you are and understanding your special talents and gifts. It is important to be clearly accepting of what you have to offer the market and the world. Your faith must follow in the same breath as knowing and understanding who you are and then you simply take the first step.

"In order to take the first step in faith, you don't have to see the whole staircase; just take the first step."

- Martin Luther King, Jr.

The action steps detailed throughout this book start when you take ownership and responsibility for your thoughts, words, actions, reactions and emotions - and finally, when you know from an intuitive standpoint the connection you are making with others. Feelings make the difference in both you and others that you encounter. Your ultimate goal must be an acute awareness of either the connections you have made or the disconnection that has taken place, which merits even greater time and attention in order to correct. Regardless of the outcome of your pursuit, your interactions will be judged by the ultimate life discriminator: how you leave them feeling!

Take a moment to reflect on how you leave people feeling after an interaction. Whether this interaction involves something as little as opening a door for a stranger or a heated argument with a coworker or spouse, how do you leave the other person feeling? Imagine you are judging the hit show American Idol. Two singers with similar talent are competing with one another to determine who will be crowned the best performer. What encourages you to vote for one performer over another? It would have to be narrowed down to how one singer, compared to another, makes you feel. When all other factors are the same, it can only be one emotional thread that makes the difference and that is how each one has left you feeling following their performances.

When you cast your final vote for the winner, it will be much like the vote you cast in life for those to whom you want to show favor. This example illustrates how leaving others feeling good can manifest into the votes or favors you gain - and, in due course, the help you receive from others.

Another key component to serving others well is how you do things. In subsequent chapters, you will learn how to position yourself to create positive situations, even in the most challenging of circumstances. You will discover how to pull the lessons from life's many losses, while throwing away the loss and being thankful for the lesson. You will become skilled at making prudent adjustments in the heat of battle in a world of shifting priorities. You will discover how to capitalize on and to spread, the benefits of building positive relationships.

You can create a word-of-mouth "epidemic" through those who support your endeavors. If you learn to perfect but one skill, become a perpetual student in the game of life and always remain focused on how you leave others feeling. When mastered, this skill alone will drive all of your other endeavors up the road to success. The sooner you master this skill, the quicker you will master the simple, yet illusive, art of realizing your dreams, living a life of purpose and accomplishing the significant aspects of your intended mission.

I have heard countless people utter the most ridiculous comments regarding basic human relations. They say things such as "I don't care if people like me or not." "I don't care what other people think of me - I know who I am." "If others don't like me, that is their problem; maybe they have the wrong perception of me." Please note, you will never be able to please all of the people all of the time. It is, however, in your best interest for people to like you, to want to hear what you have to say, to value your opinion and to want to spend time in your space and in your world.

If people have a difficult time with you, or because of you, you will never be given the opportunity of helping others get what they want. The option of serving their needs will pass you by. The law of reciprocity, sowing and reaping, sums it up nicely: first you sow and then you reap. This ageless law doesn't work in reverse: First you reap and then you sow. If you squander the chance of sowing, this of course cuts off the cycle of giving at the start. Others will never be in a position to help you get what you want, because you clearly can't get past the front door of helping them get what they want - the seed-sowing part.

Have you ever witnessed a tree growing from thin air?! Of course not. Trees grow from seeds. If you have ever enjoyed an apple or an orange, you can bet it started from the planting of a seed. Getting what you want from life starts with the exact same principle: Plant the seed, nourish and harvest its growth, then enjoy the fruits of your labor. Relationships begin in the same manner. They too, must grow from humble beginnings. The seed of any relationship begins with a hello, a handshake and an introduction. This is followed by the nourishing cycle and culminates with the harvesting of quality relationships and friendships, which bring value to our lives.

The title of this book, How You Leave Them Feeling, was born from a realization of the primary reason for my success. Whenever I consider my place in the journey to success and evaluate the gifts that have helped me, I trace their origins back to teachers, friendships, clients and conditions that were created as a direct result of how I consistently left others feeling.

I ultimately discovered that we control our own destiny, regardless of where or how we get our start in life. By learning and observing truths that have stood the test of time, I could actually plan my freedom and predict my happiness by escaping the rat race. I vowed to thrive on strong roots grounded in the following universal principles, which I call "The Seven Essential Laws of Life."

Seven Essential Laws of Life

First Essential Law of Life:
The Law of Attitude

Second Essential Law of Life:
The Law of Communication

Third Essential Law of Life:
The Law of Personal and Professional Development

Fourth Essential Law of Life:
The Law of Accumulation

Fifth Essential Law of Life:
The Law of Attraction

Sixth Essential Law of Life:
The Law of Cause and Effect

Seventh Essential Law of Life:
The Law of Balance

What connects the seven essential laws of life can be summed up in a word - feeling! The Law of Attitude deals with how you feel and how others feel about the image you portray. The Law of Communication provides the tool for leaving others feeling good. The Law of Personal and Professional Development is an extension of how well you are able to condition yourself to feel. The Law of Accumulation dictates that we feel better by accumulating growth and a better quality-of-life index over time. The Law of Attraction stimulates our feel-good glands by attracting us to that which stimulates our growth. We feel good whenever we can see the fruits of our labor through the Law of Cause and Effect. Lastly, whenever we discover the Law of Balance, everyone around us feels better.

Think of the seven essential laws as a blueprint for happiness and success. How we leave others feeling is a measure of our ability to follow the blueprint. We will examine the universal laws throughout this book and you will be given specific action steps relating to how and when to use them. They work all the time; even when you don't know they are in motion, they still work.

The game of life - a universal player's card

I have been actively involved in various facets of professional speaking for more than 16 years. My passion for helping others through education has led me to find my calling. And my clear understanding of my life's mission has stemmed from my carrying the banner of leadership. I have a strong desire to be the very best that I can be and to compete only with myself on a world scale.

The time to become a major player embracing our new global society has arrived and I will make every effort to capitalize on this opportunity. I have applied for my "card-carrying membership" in the global community and my membership has been accepted. With my universal player's card, I have enrolled in the game of developing and living the good life now. In this game, I have received a fair share of hits and I know these will manifest into a lifelong string of home runs! I practice the universal laws mentioned above and I'm determined to make them work in my life. As you learn or reaffirm these laws, you too, can significantly improve your batting average in the game of life.

Who can be helped by reading this book?

Everyone can be helped by reading this book! The student will communicate better with the teacher; the factory worker will develop a better dialogue with his colleagues; the chief executive officer will improve lines of communication with her vice presidents; fathers and daughters will break down barriers and discover avenues of rewarding dialogue. Kobe Bryant of the Los Angeles Lakers would learn to cherish the strengths of Shaquille O'Neal of the Miami Heat and embrace each of their combined gifts. Regardless of your station in life, this book will help you manage all of your relationships better. We are all complex beings and learning to help one another by making solid connections is where the true secrets of life are stored. Put another way, we learn to help ourselves by learning how to help others!

What makes this book important? It breaks down the common and tired barriers of communication. It resolves the question "Why do I have to change?" This book defines why other people's perceptions become your reality. You will be forced to think about your responsibility in maintaining good relations. If you managed yourself to the highest degree, who would you develop into on the way to discovering how to become a better person?

Ask yourself this: What kind of world would this be if everyone were just like me? Depending on your honest answer, is this a dark world or can you see light at the end of the tunnel? Is there a stadium full of light? You will be given action steps to repair or strengthen your character, image or perception and these steps will produce clearly noticeable positive differences in the short run.

Change your life by changing your thinking and by changing the company you keep

Everyone is energized by exposure to just the right light, much like the rays of the sun make us feel rejuvenated. Most people who are exposed to prolonged darkness experience unshakeable melancholy. People possessing dark natures can affect you in the same manner as not being exposed to enough sunlight.

"We learn to help ourselves by learning how to help others!"

- Jesse Ferrell

"Good habits are hard to form and easy to live with and bad habits are easy to form and hard to live with."

- Unknown

Whenever we expose ourselves to darker personality types, our feelings become negative, gloom and doom abound and we experience melancholy similar to that of being deprived of sunlight. We tend to harbor feelings of low self-esteem and suffer episodes of self-doubt. More than likely, we begin to form bad habits that don't serve us. There is a maxim I heard long ago: "Good habits are hard to form and easy to live with and bad habits are easy to form and hard to live with."

This thought helps us to understand the importance of personalities that are light in nature. People of this type tend to brighten our spirits and infuse us with renewed faith that things will get better. We become more positive and full of energy and more likely to cultivate good habits.

Have you ever experienced a time when you met someone new and, although your verbal communication was slight, you walked away feeling worse than before the encounter? If you answer yes to this question, it is quite possible you experienced the influence of bad energy. Some people who are locked into negative personality types are very aware of how they leave you feeling - toxic! Others, however, just can't seem to figure out why they move from one failed personal relationship to another. In any case, your intuition is signaling you that little or nothing can come from continued exposure to these bad-energy types. The best action step to take here is to restrict or eliminate exposure to negative personalities and toxic relationships.

At the same time, positive personality types can energize and rejuvenate us. Those who have uplifting personalities leave us feeling better after even the briefest encounters. They lighten our day. Their high spirits become welcome energy boosts, sugar for our souls - in a word, infectious. You naturally begin to feel better and become transformed into a positive-thinking person.

Positive thinking leads to positive knowing and, consequently, to positive doing.

Whenever you move from a state of apathy to a state of positive action, a cycle of benefits is just around the corner. Think of it as going to college and majoring in a discipline called "Lifestyle Enhancement 101." The key action step here is to be very selective of whom you spend your time with. Surround yourself with positive personality types whose energy transfers leave you feeling good. You need not worry about going too many times to the well of the givers of this energy, for it is in their nature to share the light. And although they put out a fair amount of energy to help you, that energy, plus some, returns to them when they see you transformed and improved by their efforts.

You will be compelled to change your thinking as a result of the above-mentioned, easy-to-execute action steps and the meaning you will extract from the vivid life stories told in the following pages. Changing your thinking in this way will yield astounding results and lead to your living the life you deserve: a life of enrichment - the good life now. I recently met the powerful professional speaker and author Brian Tracy, who shared with me his book, "Change Your Thinking, Change Your Life." Tracy reveals how to unlock your full potential for success simply by changing your thinking. I highly recommend this book for understanding the ideal that you can only achieve it when you believe it!

"Changing your life is as easy as changing your thinking."

- Brian Tracy

Planting the seed of how you leave them feeling

My intuitive nature, strong curiosity, creative streak and natural knack for organization, coaching, strategic planning, mentoring and team-building have all prepared me to deliver this book's message. My desire to give back to a system from which I have so freely taken has compelled me to share key principles of success - principles that will help you move from the sidelines of the game of life, to the spotlight, as a star performer in your own destiny!

You will discover the power of the concept how you leave them feeling and the remarkable gifts earned through honoring your commitment to leave people feeling good! You will learn customer care and customer-service models; relationship marketing strategies and common-sense guidelines to help you build your road to success. The road map to personal and professional development can be found in this book. It is devoted to empowering you to get started now and to energizing you! As you practice applying its principles, people may forget what you have done, but they will never forget how you made them feel!

My ultimate goal is to plant the seed of how you leave them feeling, while encouraging you to move forward with nothing short of a direct and immediate call-to-action. Real-life examples and simple, knowledge-based methods of operating will show you how to identify where you stand and help you make the changes you need to ensure profound success in your interactions with others.

Beware! There are doses of real-life humor and enthusiasm in the stories that follow. Should you continue reading this book, it may cause you to make profound changes - and to improve the quality of your life!

Chapter 1

Truth or Consequences of How You Leave People Feeling

Do you gain far more regret than satisfaction from your interpersonal communications? This chapter will explore the options for developing or improving your interpersonal skills. The definition of interpersonal skills, as given in Webster's New World Dictionary, is quite simple: "relating to, or involving, relations between persons." This definition encompasses all of your interpersonal relationships, from blood relatives to employers, acquaintances, friendships and intimate relationships.

You might be under the impression that because you are in love with your boyfriend or wife, you treat them differently than a good friend or close coworker. The truth is that while you may have different facets or multiple levels to your array of relationships, you are most likely bringing the same person to all of these associations.

If you tend to be a bit rough around the edges and often find yourself wearing the label of an ass, you are going to be an ass to your friend, in a platonic fashion and an ass to your loved one, in an intimate fashion. If your personality is inclined toward the nice-guy side, you will generally be a person who tends to get along with your coworkers and make peace with your loved ones. The old adage - "Wherever you go, there you are" applies here! Changing your surroundings will not change who you are: You simply bring the ass in you along for the ride. The consequences of refusing to take a strong introspective look at yourself, or taking a look and coming back with a false reading, will be the eventual doom of your interpersonal relationships.

"Wherever you go, there you are."

- Unknown

We can always tell when we have behaved poorly, even those of us who behave like an ass on a regular basis.

The first signal of behaving poorly can be read on the faces of others after your interaction with them. A feeling in the pit of your stomach signals trouble or personal unbalance. Admitting to this behavior and undertaking damage control are steps in the right direction, but they still leave plenty of room on the highway of redemption.

Many people fool themselves into believing their negative actions are warranted. This denial arises from an extremely selfish nature and the overriding objective for people like this is to get what they want at all costs. Having an egocentric nature, they never even think to treat you in a congenial fashion, which might not only lead to the satisfaction of their request, but possibly offer additional perks.

We often refuse to take ownership at critical junctures in our interpersonal relationships. Those who have advanced interpersonal skills understand when to invoke damage control measures in order to repair breaches of poor communication. This can feel unsettling, like a drive down an old, unpaved country road. But putting both hands on the wheel, taking full control and ownership and steering the car through all conditions are what creating and maintaining good relationships with others are all about. This less-traveled road is where life ultimately gets easier, as we are able to make adjustments in our interpersonal communications along the way. The reward is personal growth and improved relationships.

If you fail to take ownership for the times when you have communicated poorly and elect to continue doing what you have always done, you will perpetuate a negative cycle of leaving people feeling poorly. Personal regrets stack up and create a bone yard of failed interpersonal relationships and missed opportunities for both reward and growth. These regrets stem from denial of the truth, the truth about where we stand with our interpersonal skills.

Your fate within the relationship rests in others' perceptions of your character, your actions and your words - it comes down to how you leave them feeling. Other people's perceptions of you become your reality! You will be judged and treated in a manner consistent with what others believe about you. The truth may be an entirely different story, but people's perceptions of you are what you will be left to deal with.

"Other people's perceptions of you become your reality."

- Jesse Ferrell

Mr. Dunn: A story of how not to leave people feeling

During my years of working as a casino marketing executive in Las Vegas, Nevada, at numerous multimillion-dollar hotel and casino resorts, I encountered a broad range of interesting personalities. These unique and sometimes eccentric people always left me feeling a variety of emotions. One client stands out far and above the rest for his ability to push all the wrong buttons. He represents the epitome of behaving like an ass at all times and leaving others in a state of conflicting emotions. His rude and insensitive demands had a way of leaving my stomach in knots, whether the encounter was in person or by long distance.

The emotions that would strike simultaneously might include: fear, nervousness, resentment, revulsion and a sense of being abused. From the time I would receive Mr. Dunn's first call to book a room for a typical three-night stay, until I received his call that he had returned home safely, dealing with him was a nightmare. He was never stingy enough to reserve his abuse just for me; he made sure to spread his venom to every employee that crossed his path. He always left a trail of discontent and discord in his wake. His presence alone was enough to poison the environment.

Mr. Dunn serves as a model of how not to leave people

feeling. His story illustrates how others were left feeling as a result of his demands and greed. His behavior and quest to have things his way, regardless of who might suffer in the process, is a prime example of what not to do.

When I served as director of the casino marketing department, I always faced a peculiar dilemma in managing Mr. Dunn. He represented significant value to the company with his "high-roller" status and ability to play blackjack and baccarat. His potential losses to the casino were, on average, in the amounts of $100,000 per each three-night stay. Mr. Dunn was never worried about such losses because his day job as a Wall Street commodities broker always kept him in the green.

Whenever Mr. Dunn was not happy with the service, he would launch his verbal assaults and complaints directly to the Regional Senior Vice President of West Coast Resorts. The subsequent call coming from the Vice President of Marketing was never pleasant, as we hustled to put out whatever fire Mr. Dunn had started.

Those who dealt with this difficult client were laying their jobs on the line. The slightest mistake or simple misunderstanding would be enough incentive for him to push the panic button and make the call upstairs. In a matter of minutes, you were over a barrel. It was a helpless feeling.

Regardless of efforts to please him, nothing was ever good enough. He could not find the heart to show any appreciation. I can remember being on vacation during one of his trips and receiving an angry call from him. He was yelling at the top of his lungs because he was not happy with his $75,000 win for the trip. He was demanding full complimentary rooms, food and beverage along with airfare reimbursement for himself, his wife and two young children. Mr. Dunn had conveniently forgotten that he was already $3,000 overcompensated before the additional request of airfare reimbursement. He did not care that I was on vacation and he insisted that I make the correction regarding his full reimbursement from wherever I was at the time, or he would take his valued business elsewhere.

I can assure you, I have never taken kindly to being threatened and this type of behavior didn't make me grow an attraction for him or for managing his account. I always maintained proper decorum and class in handling Mr. Dunn, but deep inside I felt repulsed and disgusted. I couldn't afford to show it, but I grew to despise him.

The hardest part about managing hostile customers is knowing that your livelihood is on the line and that there is very little you can do about it. Mr. Dunn understood that his weight in the casino afforded him the leeway to abuse both me and any other employees he encountered. I could always bend my mind around his abuse, but I had a much tougher time stomaching the vulnerable position he put me in when it came to maintaining my livelihood.

My thoughts would constantly return to the fact that Mr. Dunn's actions were always calculated - he knew what position he was placing me in. It was as though he reveled in the power of being able to control me by toying with my emotions. The challenge of unscrambling my emotions burned like rubbing alcohol in an open wound. Managing Mr. Dunn was like walking around with Faberge eggs in a weak basket and, with a sense of impending doom, knowing that the eggs would eventually shatter all over the floor. He was well aware of how he left me feeling and never showed an ounce of remorse.

Many of you know someone just like Mr. Dunn. But have you ever figured out how to manage such people? Were you ever able to determine what you should learn from such extreme challenges?

Learning how not to behave with others

Among other key lessons, we learn how not to behave, how not to treat others. We learn that people who make such a production out of toying with the emotions and livelihoods of others are bitter, unhappy people. These people believe they may relieve their own stress, internal pain or demons by making our lives miserable.

The old misery-loves-company game is at work here. A quote from my friend James Catledge (Founder and CEO of Impact Net Worth) seems appropriate here. James says people like Mr. Dunn "read by the lamp of their own conceit." The consequences for people who persist in conducting themselves in this manner, without any correction, usually manifest in a number of ways. They may find themselves playing the role of social misfits, shunned by friends, family and business relations. Oftentimes, the only people with whom they are able to surround themselves are those who typically work in service-oriented roles. Thus they are ultimately paying for the attention that is awarded them. They often end up with all sorts of illnesses before dying lonely.

People like Mr. Dunn can invoke negative emotions in you and bring out a side that you may never have known you had. Imagine finding yourself begging for instant justice or seeking revenge. But in the long run, these tactics will not help you feel any better about being subjected to abusive behavior. If not managed properly, frustration and repressed anger can gnaw at you and leave you feeling bitter. Observing the first set of action steps that follow will provide avenues for effectively managing these challenging emotional issues and leave the justice up to a higher court.

If you are unfortunate enough to have a personality

like Mr. Dunn's, I hope his story hits home with you and offers you a mirror for self-examination. You may finally understand how your character and actions consistently leave others feeling. I hope true introspection would lead to your seeking help in order to rid yourself of destructive character flaws. The second set of action steps below will assist you in managing your characteristics and behaviors that are similar to Mr. Dunn's.

Key Action Steps
Truth or Consequences of
How You Leave People Feeling

Dealing with difficult people or
personality types like Mr. Dunn's

Action Step 1
Maintain your integrity and self-respect

In spite of the peculiar intentions of a character like Mr. Dunn, always maintain your integrity and self-respect. Never give in and allow difficult people to crush your spirit. You will find that you gain respect in the eyes of difficult people when they discover that their roguish and subversive tactics don't leave you flat-lined.

Action Step 2
Minimize your exposure

A clear and easy way to manage difficult personality types is to minimize your exposure to people who fit this profile. As simple as this sounds, it may not come to you straightaway that restricting the time you spend with hard-to-stomach personality types just may be the key to managing them in the long run. You don't want this to be noticeable, so your method of taking control of your exposure should be adjusted based on the individual personalities and the specific circumstances.

Action Step 3
Neutralize negative energy

Positive self-talk will assist in balancing your mental environment whenever you are interacting with difficult people. Your natural inclination may be to respond negatively, at least mentally, to the negative energy coming your way. Holding positive thoughts, however, can be a strong weapon to neutralize the negative energy of others as you interact with them.

Action Step 4
Search for tidbits of positive traits

Even those with caustic personalities have something positive about them. Always search for those tidbits of good things about difficult people or, at the very least, find the lesson and throw everything else away. If you have exhausted your search for good traits about a difficult person, you can still search for the lesson in having to interact with them and this can be the positive redeeming quality about dealing with them.

Action Step 5
Remember to give because you enjoy helping others

Many times you may find yourself becoming cynical or resentful at having to get along with difficult people. This, of course, could quickly make you want to shut down your nature of giving. Remember, you are giving because you enjoy helping others; don't let another's abusive nature taint your ability to give; refuse to regret giving.

**Managing your own negative characteristics
or behaviors**

Action Step 1
Monitor the reactions of others

As you look to improve the quality of your interactions
with others, increase your awareness of how others are
reacting to you. By adding this invaluable resource to
your communication ideal, you allow yourself plenty
of time for course correction. If you perceive that you
are hitting people the wrong way and their acknowl-
edgement or body language is confirming this, make the
needed positive changes immediately.

Action Step 2
Practice counter-intuitive measures

If you tend to rub others the wrong way or constantly
find yourself on the bad side of others, practicing counter-intuitive measures will serve as a marvelous dam-
age-prevention tool. In other words, if your natural
behaviors and reactions are garnering poor results, try
behaving counter to your natural inclination. For example, if you are typically slow to smile whenever you open
the communication process with others, change this by
initiating the first smile.

If you typically wait until people warm up to you before
talking to them, start launching into conversation first
in a warm and friendly fashion. These subtle counter-
intuitive changes may be all that are needed to keep
your communication with others on the positive side.

Action Step 3
Preprogram yourself for positive responses

Your negative nature just may be the culprit that creates others' poor perception of you and lets your character in for a beating. A good way to compensate for

a negative nature is to preprogram yourself to respond positively before you encounter others. This comes as easily as saying, "I'm going to respond positively during my next interaction, regardless of the nature of the conversation." People can sense whether your character tends to be positive or negative in nature. As I mentioned earlier, positive thinking transforms into positive doing!

Action Step 4
Check others' perceptions of you

A checkup from the neck up will help you understand how others perceive your actions and intentions. This simply involves consulting with a confidant regarding the quality of your behavior and interactions with others. Determine if others' perceptions of you and your intentions are matching up.

Action Step 5
Remember to be kind

Oftentimes, people who have a character similar to that of Mr. Dunn feel like they must always convince others of how well-informed and how right they are all of the time. Remember, it is always better to be kind than to be right. Always take care to gauge the times when it's necessary to present your knowledge in order to help a situation improve.

If you find yourself interacting with someone and the matter is not one of urgency or liability and others with whom you are communicating may have trouble handling a prudently investigated point of view, resist the urge to press the issue. Rather than getting cheers for bringing your knowledge to the table, you could likely end up with resentment instead of gratitude. Elect to forgo being right and opt for being kind.

Summary Points

Truth or Consequences of How You Leave People Feeling

1. Learn to discover and to live with personal satisfaction - versus personal regret - about how you leave others feeling

2. Face the truth of your disposition head-on and help shape the outcome of your actions, rather than being surprised by the consequences

3. Make a definitive motion toward sharing positive energy with others and measure their reactions as you are interacting with them

4. Never place yourself in a position where you are seeking justice from those who poison your environment with their negative energy

5. Practice counter-intuitive measures to balance your disposition when you are engaged with negative-energy types

Affirmations
Moments for Reflection

1. I read people very well and sense where they are coming from within minutes of meeting them

2. All of my interactions are positive or strong life experiences

3. I am an excellent listener and my relationships are improved because of this

4. I am now drawing to me positive people and rewarding circumstances

5. I seek out and welcome people with positive energy into my life

Chapter 2

Leaving Your Signature is a Measure of How You Do Things

Difficult people place hardships on themselves and others. They generally have personal regrets rather than personal satisfaction. Instead of settling for a life of causing havoc and unhappiness to others, take the high road and choose to make a positive difference in the lives of others. The truth is we are only one handshake away from an entirely different lifestyle. The consequences will result from doing the right thing by that handshake or from losing a golden opportunity because of lackluster or poor behavior.

Growing your network of relationships ultimately becomes a rewarding responsibility. Your personal and professional endeavors are strengthened exponentially by understanding the value of shaking the hand of someone new - by leaving others feeling good as the stamp of your personal signature.

Your signature represents your unique style and it's the manner in which you do things that others come to know you for. Leaving your signature with someone is like leaving a wonderful scent behind. Have you ever been in the presence of someone who puts on just the right amount of cologne and after they have left the room, you smell a hint of their pleasant fragrance? You could make a similar mark by having a pleasant personality and sharing it with others. This is what I mean by leaving your personal signature behind. I wrote an article sometime ago, called "Footprints In the Heart," which mirrors this signature concept in many ways:

FOOTPRINTS IN THE HEART!

Do you leave your personal signature on EVERY-THING you do? Have you left a footprint in the heart of EVERYONE you touch?

How do you do things?

Are you the kind of person who holds back your energy and talent, saving your best performance for just the right time? Then BAM! Waalah, you roll into action and give 'em your best shot - one swing of the bat and it's a home run out of the park! You saved the day! Feels great, doesn't it? What a way to leave a footprint in the hearts and minds of all your teammates!

But wait, what's behind that performance? Do you sit back waiting for that moment to shine? Or do you invest part of every day preparing for it?

We've all heard the expression "practice makes perfect." Baseball's legendary super slugger Barry Bonds adds a twist to that old expression that we all know is true: "Perfect practice makes practice perfect."

So what do these expressions suggest about how we should be doing things?

Not even the strongest major league baseball slugger comes to the plate, takes one swing and hits home run after home run. He spends all his time preparing for that moment - every day of his life.

Imagine Bonds, likely baseball's all time best home run hitter. How many times does he strike out in his quest to belt that ball over the fence? What is his pre-game preparation? Does he show up for practice late and leave early? How important might weight training, or a diet program, or mental or spiritual balancing, be in his quest for that next home run?

Indeed, a man like Bonds is in constant preparation for that next stellar home run. As sure as day and night, he is focused on preparation as though every game were the World Series. He will visualize himself in the batter's box with the winning run resting upon his ability to swing the bat with efficiency. He will hit that home run hundreds of times in his mind before ever actually finding himself at bat in a live, prime-time situation. And, during both practice and performance, he will inevitably leave his signature - his footprint - on everything he does.

Consider Bonds as an example of preparation and execution in your own life plan. Visualize everything you do as though you are playing ball in the major leagues. You have both the opportunity and responsibility to do your best - all the time.

Challenge yourself to upgrade your signature style; give your Customer Service Package a face-lift! Those around you will feel it and this will help to further increase your own productivity. This is the Law of Reciprocity. I have heard it said, "When you help others get what they want, they will help you get what you want." Start this practice with the very next person you come into contact with after reading this article. Give them a genuine smile, engage them in conversation and look for an opening through which you may wow them by leaving a footprint in their hearts.

You will be amazed at how easy these few simple ideas are to do and how they will change your life in a powerful way! After putting them to work, don't be surprised if you find yourself hitting those balls out of the park, not just once in a while - but every single day!

Choose to develop your personal power

You can develop or strengthen your personal power as a matter of choice. Have you ever wondered what people think and say about you when you are not present? Behaving in a positive and giving manner will not guarantee that you are spoken of favorably. However, if you focus on creating a pleasing signature, others will most likely be inclined to feel positively about you. At the very least, you should never be accused of being difficult to deal with or of behaving poorly.

Developing personal power is the sign of true leadership. And leadership is influence. Should you already have a style such as this, or if you are looking to enhance or develop a pleasant signature, I'll bet you would be more inclined to chalk up personal satisfaction points versus personal regrets for your efforts. Your personal power supports your character and lives on long after you have left the room. You become very memorable to others when you are resonating personal power. Consequently, both personal power and becoming memorable to others will help create bargaining power as your leadership capability grows.

You are only one handshake away from an entirely different lifestyle

All of the best relationships start from a simple introduction or handshake. The harvesting of good friendships could not be possible without the fostering of new relationships. The author of "The Craving Brain", Dr. Ronald Ruden, notes that we are herd animals. We enjoy congregating in groups. He makes the point that we enjoy being around those we consider to be like ourselves. Hence, this is the reason for country club memberships, ethnic neighborhoods, religious communities, Alcoholics Anonymous and the like. He further stresses that other species also believe in this herding concept; that's why there are schools of fish, flocks of geese, herds of wildebeest and endless other herding or flocking species.

The philosophy behind the herding concept is not so

much for protection against others who are not like us; it is to help us know that there are others like us around. This lowers our stress level. A lowering of stress in situations like this translates into a lowering of our dopamine levels. In this case, dopamine is the simple amino acid that the brain releases during times of stress, which in turn switches on our fight or flight mechanism. Operating in a lower-stress environment relieves us of stressful situations and makes us calmer. This allows us to make better connections with both strangers and people we know. It creates the potential for heightened interpersonal relationships, which is fertile ground for synergy. The emergent synergy between contacts is the best formula for receiving maximum benefits through interpersonal relationship building. These benefits manifest themselves in terms of lasting friendships, partnerships, alliances and limitless business opportunities.

Furthermore, developing synergies creates what I call the "compounding effect." This effect works much like compounding interest on a mutual fund. The power of investing in mutual funds and realizing compounding interest, versus simply leaving your money in the bank at less than one percent, is what makes the savvy investor wealthy over time! This same principle is at work when you invest in the compounding effect and its relationship to opportunities that translate into a high quality of life. The handshake theory is just as simple as it sounds; every hand that you shake is potentially a life-changing opportunity.

The opportunity to shake the most hands increases when we respect the naturally occurring herding instinct. This results in lowered stress and more connections being made. The time you spend building quality relationships to support your life's mission will be reduced as a result of the connections made through the people you know and through the people they know.

The key to the compounding effect is discovered when

your connections introduce you to the people they know with enthusiasm and full support of you. Think of the compounding effect much like reaping the reward of an investment that has outperformed the S&P 500 over the past 20 years. You not only earn additional dollars with such an investment, but you also earn influence and bargaining power. Thus the compounding effect is like building influence and bargaining power. Your attitude will be a key determinant in sustaining the synergy built between contacts and friends, which will truly leave them feeling good!

Creating a word-of-mouth "epidemic" to cause your business and relationships to tip in your favor

Malcolm Gladwell, author of "The Tipping Point", describes something closely related to the compounding effect: a phenomenon that he calls "the strength of weak ties." Gladwell tells the story of a business that tips from certain death to a company of great prominence. In this fascinating account, readers are led through an exploration of companies that fit this profile.

The key to what caused the businesses to tip from disaster to fortune is revealed. The point is made that mavens and connectors are the catalysts for such tipping points. Webster's New World Dictionary defines a maven as "an expert or connoisseur." Gladwell defines a connector as "someone who has strong influence and bargaining power and who is well connected." Connectors know people who know groups of other people. The power of knowing groups of other people who are inclined to spread the word creates what he calls a word-of-mouth epidemic. This epidemic is the vehicle that drives the success of a business to the tipping point.

When scores of people are encouraged to buy your goods and services as a matter of recommendation, it's a short time before you are blessed with the compounding effect of inbound marketing versus outside marketing. Simply keeping up with supply and demand becomes the concern of the day. This is a problem all business owners would love to manage.

The compounding effect is similar to the word-of-mouth epidemic in that it creates influence. Most of us have heard the axiom, "there is strength in numbers." Gladwell's theory and the compounding effect signify that along with strength in numbers, the strength of weak ties can also make you a fortune! The power to grow, develop and prosper can be found in the throngs of people you don't know and may never meet.

Developing synergy and creating a mastermind alliance

After spending some time developing and maintaining a number of relationships with mavens and connectors, you will be in the perfect position to take advantage of the power of those relationships. You do this by creating a "mastermind alliance." The concept of a mastermind alliance has been around for many years.

I first discovered this concept from the best-selling book by Napoleon Hill called "Think and Grow Rich". Hill tells the story of meeting the wealthy Dale Carnegie in 1908. Carnegie wanted to employ Hill, but refused to pay him a salary. Carnegie promised that the work Hill would do for him would make him a wealthy man many times over. The work consisted of writing an economic philosophy about people of greatness, such as Henry Ford and Carnegie himself. The work was derived from numerous interviews, over a 20-year period.

The successful experiences of these famous men allow the common person to make use of their knowledge. Ultimately, Hill created a mastermind alliance from the many introductions from Carnegie and through the interviewing process.

Consistently developing synergy through your contacts places you in the position of creating the best master-mind alliance from your mavens and connectors. As noted earlier, it is the careful observation and nurturing of a positive attitude that sets the tone for creating synergy among people. You will learn more about the Law of Attitude in the following chapter. The action steps below will help you strengthen your ability to develop synergy. You will learn to leave your signature behind and create a positive word-of-mouth epidemic.

Key Action Steps
Leaving Your Signature Is a Measure of How You Do Things

Action Step 1
Take advantage of every opportunity to leave your signature behind

When you take advantage of every opportunity to leave your signature on your endeavors and with people you meet, you place yourself in an extraordinary group of people. This group is few in number. Your work and actions stand for themselves. Others come to expect quality results and coveted relationships whenever you are involved. This is an excellent way to leave others feeling. Maintaining this single virtue of a strong signature will be an insurance blanket for building quality relationships, which ultimately manifest into choices and opportunities.

Action Step 2
Choose to develop your personal power

Developing your personal power directly translates into improving your leadership qualities. As noted earlier, leadership is influence. Whenever you can influence others, your ability to positively affect people and environments becomes priceless.

Action Step 3
Live by the theory of one handshake away from an entirely different lifestyle

In order to improve or change your lifestyle, you must improve the quality of your connections. Making better connections creates the opportunity for developing synergy and this synergy increases your quality of life. Synergy is the seed for the compounding effect that creates positive results. All of this begins with a handshake or an introduction. Since we aren't aware of where introductions will take us, always treat them with respect in order to plant the right seeds for success.

Action Step 4
Create a word-of-mouth epidemic to cause your business and relationships to tip

The best form of advertising is word-of-mouth. When you associate yourself with mavens and connectors, they will help you create a word-of-mouth epidemic. The story of Paul Revere is an excellent example of the creation of a word-of-mouth epidemic. In 1775, Revere rode from Charlestown to the town of Lexington, stopping in every village along the way to warn the townsmen that the British troops were coming.

This word-of-mouth epidemic was obviously very important to the war efforts of the Americans. The mavens and connectors that you team up with can create the same type of word-of-mouth epidemic and cause your business or relationships to tip in your favor.

Action Step 5
Develop synergies and create a mastermind alliance

Following the execution of Action Step 4 above, you are now in the position to create a mastermind alliance. Your mastermind alliance will serve as your key support group to aid in your development. This alliance will be the largest determinant of your overall success and goal attainment. You must remain in constant contact with this group to ensure that your connection to members remains alive and consultation continues.

Summary Points

Leaving Your Signature Is a Measure of How You Do Things

1. Take advantage of every opportunity to leave your signature behind

2. Choose to develop your personal power by using your natural talents

3. Embrace the one handshake away from an entirely different lifestyle theory

4. Create a word-of-mouth epidemic and cause your relationships to tip in your favor

5. Develop relationship synergy and create a master mind alliance

Affirmations
Moments for Reflection

1. My personal signature is highly evolved; I attract special people into my life

2. My leadership style positively influences the lives of others every day

3. My positive outlook on life manifests good working synergy

4. All of my relationships support the optimistic world in which I live

5. I speak to members of my mastermind alliance every day, giving and receiving encouragement

Chapter 3

The First Essential Law of Life
The Law of Attitude

This chapter is dedicated to Norma and Charles Meeks from Orlando, Florida. They are the goodwill ambassadors of the Law of Attitude. If you were to bump into Charles and Norma on the street, you would not immediately take in the depth of their kindness. Despite their steady and pleasant natures, they wouldn't stand out in terms of their looks or attitude. They have the ability to blend into the crowd. This blending quality, however, is a cover for what lies just beneath the surface. They are angels in disguise. They have made a life out of unselfishly helping others. This sincere kindness and liberal spreading of goodwill is what has given them their wings and makes them special. We will learn more about the Meeks' later in this chapter.

The Law of Attitude is the first of seven essential laws of life, because your attitude is the command central for the communication process. Your ability to make positive connections with others will largely be based on your attitude and the perception others have of it. The Law of Attitude is the great connection between how you affect people you meet and your ability to leave them feeling good as a result of your interactions. In order to position yourself for success in life, you must begin with your attitude. I must make three key points before we move forward:

The Law of Attitude: three key points

1. Your attitude ultimately determines your altitude

2. Attitude affects your aura, which eventually determines boundaries

3. Extended boundaries allow maximum growth on your journey of success

Attitude determines altitude

Your attitude ultimately determines your altitude. Think of it this way: if you maintain a poor mental attitude, you will deny yourself the opportunity to climb to new heights.

Think of an eagle, one of nature's magnificent creatures, as it soars high above the ground. There are several reasons an eagle will soar to new heights. First, it has a better view of what is below. Second, if it were to fly very low to the ground, it would have to work harder to avoid trees, buildings - even the land itself. Third, it has options: it can go higher if need be, or it can descend to lower levels, but it never compromises its position. You must strive to keep your positioning - your edge. What this means to you is, do not hold yourself back from soaring higher because you have the wrong mental attitude.

In the game of life, you must sometimes accept that the playing field in which you are competing in may not be level. However, you can change things in your favor by maintaining a positive mental attitude. A key step in this process is to seek and consistently discover the good in all of your interactions. This will shore up a strong and positive outlook.

A bad attitude, whether it is justified or not, will squash your opportunities and eliminate you from the game. As they say, in order to protect against being denied opportunities in life, you should always keep your feet at the gaming table. Don't let a bad attitude put you on the outside with people who matter!

Don't let your attitude restrict the height to which you can grow - it can become an altitude wrecker! It is noteworthy to mention that so many things in our daily lives change when we change our attitude. For example, you are driving home from a long day at work and someone cuts you off in traffic. Most of us would respond aggressively and become agitated. We may think, "Perfect, this tops a day like this." But if you sit back and change your attitude, does it mean the end of the world? Perhaps not and you needn't be quite so angry. In the end, you will find your day not so bad after all.

Take one moment every day and sincerely ask yourself, "How would things change if I rose above this and changed my attitude?" You will be very surprised at what you find. You might discover that slowing down and allowing the aggressive driver to pull in front of you was just what you needed to realize that you had been speeding. The intruder was a wake-up call that saved you from a certain speeding ticket from the highway patrolman who was hiding under the overpass you quickly happened upon. How would this discovery leave you feeling?

Your attitude affects your aura

Your attitude affects your aura, which ultimately determines your boundaries. First, what is your aura? Your aura is that aspect of you that you give off without any particular actions or words. It is your general being. By the way, your aura plays a major role in the concept mentioned earlier of leaving your scent or signature behind.

We all have an aura. It is a perceived aspect of ourselves

in the world around us. Is there someone in your life that you just like being around, or someone at work you cannot stand being with, even if they say nothing at all? These feelings and emotions come from that person's aura. Obviously, it is a boon to have a good aura. Thus, having a good attitude is important. People are drawn to those with good auras and avoid those with bad ones. Your aura can vary as your attitude is modified by circumstances of life. It is best to be aware of this so that you can tap into your internal barometer of knowing. Shape your attitude and make the proper adjustments to maintain a positive aura in light of unforeseen circumstances. As we previously touched upon, possessing a good aura is also closely related to having good energy.

Whoopi Goldberg and Muhammad Ali can leave you feeling good

An awesome example of someone with good energy, a good aura and the ability to consistently leave you feeling good is Whoopi Goldberg, the actress and comedian. I met her in 2003 and it took about two minutes for me to fall in love with her aura and become totally fascinated by her energy! After speaking to her for about thirty minutes, I felt like we were kindred spirits. Whoopi Goldberg best represents the model of what I call a much-evolved soul possessing a magnificent aura. Her energy level resonates at a high velocity, but oddly enough, she seems always in control of her thoughts and emotions.

Whenever I am speaking with Whoopi Goldberg, whether it is to nurture our friendship or to relate to her as a valued JessTalk client, she always has just the right take on a range of subjects. She makes everyone around her relax and get the most out of the conversation and the experience. Her style is down-to-earth and very much matter-of-fact. As her aura reflects, she is the most evolved person I have had the pleasure of meeting.

The only other well-known personality that I have met and served in a similar capacity is Muhammad Ali. He, too, possesses a much-evolved energy level and you can feel it whether he says anything or not! Interacting with Whoopi Goldberg and Muhammad Ali always caused my energy levels to peak. I was aware that I, too, was resonating at higher energy levels as a result of the interactions. I walked away from every encounter with each of them feeling good. If there were ever to be poster children for the concept of how you leave them feeling, these two shining personalities would be the ideal subjects.

Extended boundaries allow for maximum growth on your journey of success

With a positive aura, you not only extend your boundaries, but you also undergo extreme personal growth in your new limitless realm. To expand your horizons and to grow as a human being, work together as the key to your success. If you keep your boundaries where they are, you must ask yourself, have I achieved the goals that I want with these boundaries? If you answered no, how can you expect to have goal achievement without exceeding those boundaries? The answer is you cannot have that expectation. Growth thus helps ensure that your journey of success is the most productive one possible. You will make far stronger connections with a broader range of people. This extended range will dramatically enhance your chances of getting what you want out of life. The law of averages will prevail: The more quality relationships you form as a result of the extended boundaries, the more opportunities you have for leaving others feeling good about you.

Expanding your boundaries, sometimes called "going beyond your comfort zone" - is a great way for opening yourself up to new successes. If you are to expect new and different things, your attitude must be one that will accept these changes. The point to be taken here is this: If you want something to happen, but deep down inside you do not believe it can happen for you, it never will. Opening and extending your boundaries will allow for your growth and for the success you deserve.

The power of believing is your greatest key to the most meaningful accomplishments. Author Claude M. Bristol wrote an excellent book called "The Magic of Believing", in which he gives a detailed account of the powers of belief. A friend recommended this book to me during a casual dinner engagement and I have read it a minimum of five times per year ever since. "The Magic of Believing" will either renew or broaden your perspective on the keys to a world of unlimited opportunity.

This book will release powerful forces locked in your mind, while turning desire into reality. You will learn how to use your thoughts to make things happen and adjust your attitude to get what you want out of life! The final treasure you will discover is how to leave yourself feeling, in order to develop, grow and prosper.

Being able to harness the power of belief is the cornerstone of maintaining a positive attitude and outlook. It is clearly this power that allows for the healthiest attitudes in serving others and leaving them feeling good. The following story exemplifies the effects of having a positive attitude, which is a true measure of how you leave others feeling.

A mother's love: just one more time before I die

A few years ago I received a call from an old college buddy, who also happens to be a former high school sports rival of mine. It was nice to hear from him and at the close of a three-hour conversation, we shared highlights of each others' lives over the past six years.

Just before our good-byes he said, "Oh! Yes! There is one other reason why I called you tonight. I feel really bad having to ask you this question after not being in touch for so long, however, time is of essence and I really must ask..."

I, of course, encouraged him to feel comfortable asking the question, because whatever it was, I would be more than happy to do all in my power to support him.

Faltering a bit, he continued: "Well my mother is dying of cancer and has been diagnosed with just two weeks left to live. And you know, Jess, she has been a solid go-to person for me; she's my anchor in life. I love her very much! And, well, when I sat with her today, I asked her: 'Mother, is there anything in the world that you always wanted and never had that I can get you before you pass away? Anything that you wanted to do and never did that I can help you to experience? Please tell me what I can do, because I love you so much and I want you to have it.'"

His mother paused just for a moment and said, "If I could see Jesse Ferrell just one more time before I die, that would be great."

Now, remember, I haven't seen either of them or spoken to them in more than six years. She went on to say, "Jesse's positive attitude helped me so much, whenever I was around him during your college days and during my transition to this big city of Las Vegas. That would truly make me happy...if I could see Jesse, just one more time!"

I was overwhelmed with emotion to learn how I had made his mother feel so long ago. During our college years, she had not given any indication that she felt this way. My heart sunk to my knees upon taking in her last request - I felt so deeply compassionate. I also felt honored to be part of her final wishes. In this way, she left me feeling good, which is a direct credit to how I had left her feeling. This is reminiscent of the movie "Pay It Forward", starring Kevin Spacey, in which strangers were encouraged to perform extraordinary feats of kindness for no other reason than their desire to help others and make a difference in their lives.

At this point in the conversation, it was approaching midnight and I said to my friend, "Do you want me to hang up the phone right now and get to your mother's side, or would tomorrow morning be soon enough?" I didn't want to lose this opportunity of granting her sole wish! We agreed that the following morning at 8:00 a.m. would work best for his mom.

Upon my entering the mother's home, my friend's sister scurried ahead of us and got her mother ready. I was anxiously waiting in the family room, full of excitement and anticipation to see her and surprise her. I couldn't wait to see the look on her face! It made me feel as though I had achieved celebrity status.

Although the audience on hand was small in number - her grandchildren, her son, daughter and son-in-law - they represented all who were precious to her. Although she had other family still living (husband, brothers and sisters, cousins, aunts and uncles), she had restricted visits during this critical time to only those present in the room. I was overwhelmed to be invited into that tight inner circle. This encounter has remained a personal highlight of all of my life's work to date, for it brought out feelings that I didn't know existed.

When I rounded the corner to her bedroom and she focused on me, she yelled out, "Jesse!" She smiled really warmly! Her smile melted into uncontrollable laughter! There were a lot of teeth showing between the two of us! And the rest of the family joined in the laugh-fest!

That moment will stay with me for the rest of my life! We talked for a couple of hours. I brought pictures of her son and me during our college days and a few shots of vacations that I had taken with my wife, leading up to the home we currently live in. She seemed full of life and so happy; she expressed to me what a dynamic and energizing effect I had on her life. She confided that my positive attitude had helped her in more ways than she could say. I humbly thanked her and showed the joy I had received by her pleasant, motherly style. We kissed and parted company.

Later, I received a call from my friend at work. He noted that he had not seen his mother happier since she had been diagnosed with cancer. She looked and felt alive! She wanted to go outside for a walk! She wanted to soak in the rays of the sun! She was positively different all day long! I was ecstatic about the update; it gave me hope for her survival and made me feel proud that my healthy attitude had helped her in some way. It was empowering to know that I could still leave her feeling good!

I placed a call on the second day and she had been moved to a hospice. I spoke to her a couple times over the next couple of days. I discovered that she loved cookies and my wife just happens to be the "world's best cookie baker," so I naturally promised to bring her a dozen of Teresa's finest T Cookies! When I called the following day to determine the best time to deliver the cookies, my friend's mother had passed away. But she left behind such a good feeling and new sense of awareness in me.

"You should always be willing to give what you can to others; sometimes it is far more than you think."

- Unknown

My positive attitude had moved something in my friend's mom and sustained her favorable emotions about me over the years. Beyond that, her strong spirit inspired me to take my sensitivity and positive attitude to another level! I am eternally grateful for this gift! I have heard it said, "You should always be willing to give what you can to others; sometimes, it is far more than you think!" This story supports my belief that you should always remain compassionate with others while sharing your gifts.

Using the Law of Attitude to improve personal and professional relationships

Adhering to the Law of Attitude will improve your personal and professional relationships. As you continue to polish up your attitude, be prepared to find your aura and energies resonating at higher levels, such as those of Whoopi Goldberg and Muhammad Ali.

Whenever I'm working with my JessTalk clients, we analyze the client's attitude, studying how it applies to his or her life. We are able to adjust for new and better relationships by working on improving the client's attitude. Whenever my clients aren't sure about how their attitudes may be portrayed to the world, I offer the counsel of less is more. When in doubt, leave it out.

You can almost always re-enter a situation and deliver added messages. However, once you have delivered a message and it is either wrong or inappropriate, you can never take it back and people never forget your indiscretion. I often hear people say this person or that person has a "really bad attitude - they need to lighten up." The dilemma is that even though many times we are able to identify a problem, we are unaware of the cascading effects it has on our lives and the lives of others. Hence, we are not always quick to adjust our attitudes. Understanding these effects will dramatically improve how we make attitude adjustments and enhance the way in which our attitude leaves others feeling about us.

Can you recall a time when you could have used the Law of Attitude to improve a situation? Perhaps it was a time when you exercised your quick tongue and delivered a few burning words when a softer, more elevated tone would have been far more appropriate and beneficial for everyone involved.

Sometimes, you only need to think before you act and you find the desired results come a great deal more easily. We all find ourselves at times in life wanting to react quickly. We may want to right a wrong or to strike back, but when have those actions ever truly resulted in accomplishing any desired results? By remaining respectful to the Law of Attitude and ensuring that you do not let opportunities to use this law pass you by, your journey will be significantly strengthened.

The story of Charles and Norma Meeks - it's your attitude I'm attracted to

The Law of Attitude is far reaching and crosses paths with the six other essential laws of life. Your ability to successfully follow the remaining laws will be heavily impacted by how well you manage the Law of Attitude, which requires consistent application throughout all facets of your life. When clearly focusing on this law, the journey of life becomes much easier and more enjoyable. A particular story comes to mind about Charles and Norma Meeks; it is an example of reaping the benefits of maintaining a good attitude at all times. As the goodwill ambassadors for the Law of Attitude, the Meeks' move through life continually adjusting their attitudes to get the most out of life.

I met Charles and Norma Meeks in a most interesting manner. It was during a time period when I was working as a casino marketing executive and serving clients during a very hectic period. I was unaware that Norma had been observing me closely as I worked feverishly in a room full of impatient clients. Norma later informed me that she wanted to befriend me because she had been enamored by observing the quality of my attitude as I worked to serve some very difficult clients. Please do not miss the moral of the story here: They chose me well before I had an opportunity to choose them. Of course, as I have come to know them now, I would have chosen them first, in a heartbeat! The initial professional relationship we formed has grown into several different parallel relationships. We have traveled out of the country on vacation together; we have spent time in one another's homes. I have done work for their businesses and they have fully supported my professional speaking company, JessTalk Speaking Services.

During the time that I first met the Meeks', it never occurred to me that we would become such an integral part of one another's lives. I wasn't aware that they represented the philosophy of one handshake away from an entirely different lifestyle. We formed a series of new and blossoming relationships. I have had the opportunity to bond with each of their family members and to participate in each of their lives. I have done everything from speaking to their daughter's high school class about life development, to fishing on the open seas in the Bahamas with Charles Meeks, to participating as a member of the wedding party in their younger son's wedding.

When you consider the circumstances in which I first met this family, it is apparent that having just the right positive attitude pays off. It brought me the entire Meeks family (Nicole, Ryan, Eric, April, Garrett, Mana, Cody, Katrina, Dylan, Dalton) of lifelong friendships! I think of them as friends and family first; but they remain top JessTalk clients, always extending full support to my company and its growth.

There can be no higher moral of any story than that which upholds the need to acquire quality lasting friendships through the process of sharing a positive attitude and the desire to make a difference in the lives of others. The example of the Meeks family serves as a model for the first essential law of life, the Law of Attitude. The

Meeks' are the bonus gift received from the Law of Attitude and the notion of how you leave them feeling! The action steps below will help you strengthen the Law of Attitude in your life.

Key Action Steps
The Law of Attitude

Action Step 1
Identify how you are projecting to others

A checkup from the neck up will increase the quality of your perspective with regard to both your attitude and aura. The best way to accomplish this is by using an impartial confidant who can offer evaluation and respectful criticism when and where needed. The number-one mission for this confidant is to help monitor how you are projecting to others - in short, how others perceive your intentions. Your ability to make adjustments based on this valuable input will keep your character polished.

Action Step 2
Harness the power of belief

"People always do the things they view as important; if they aren't doing them, it is because they don't view them as important."

- Unknown

The power of belief is critical to connecting the right thoughts to the best actions. As sure as day follows night in a perpetual cycle, your thoughts follow your belief system. As your belief system is strengthened, your thoughts are positively affected and what you think about grows. You are naturally inclined to take action on those thoughts you view as important. A client once shared this quote with me: "People always do the things they view as important; if they aren't doing them, it is because they don't view them as important!" This is why the power of belief becomes your greatest key to the most meaningful accomplishments.

Action Step 3
Remain respectful and compassionate with others

We are all blessed with certain gifts. Some of us are musically inclined, while others may be artistic, athletic or excellent at communicating. Regardless of your gift, you should always remain respectful and compassionate when sharing your gifts with others. The communication process will be heightened when observing an attitude of humility. The legion of well-wishers will grow as you mature. You are bound to leave them feeling good when you practice humility.

Action Step 4
Attitude: when in doubt, leave it out

Many of us invariably find ourselves in situations where we may be unsure of how to react to peculiar circumstances. Our attitudes can become infected, either by unique circumstances or odd people. When reacting, it thus becomes important to use a measure of prudence: When in doubt, leave it out. This is the motto I recommend. It is far easier to revisit a situation and provide additional messages than it is to take back a wrongful or inappropriate remark stemming from an attitude glitch.

Summary Points
The First Essential Law of Life:
The Law of Attitude

1. Checkup from the neck up - identify how you are projecting to others

2. The power of belief - your thoughts create your actions

3. Remain compassionate with others while sharing your gifts

4. In terms of attitude, when in doubt leave it out

5. Extending your boundaries is the key to decisive success

Affirmations
Moments for Reflection

1. I radiate positive energy and my personal signature continues to evolve

2. I refresh my thoughts with daily reading and meditation exercises

3. My compassion for helping others allows me to apply my gifts

4. I am constantly improving my attitude, which refreshes and energizes me

5. My personal and professional boundaries continue to grow on a daily basis

Chapter 4

The Second Essential Law of Life
The Law of Communication

The second essential law of life, the Law of Communication, is part of a natural progression that follows from the Law of Attitude. In fact, it would be difficult to talk about the Law of Communication without further reference to the Law of Attitude. The Law of Communication and the Law of Attitude are clear synergistic partners working very closely together. They are often present at the same time, impacting one another. Your willingness to harness and utilize the Law of Communication will be powerful once put into action with the Law of Attitude.

The power of a positive attitude creates the energy that flows through the pipeline of the Law of Communication. The synergistic work of the Law of Attitude and the Law of Communication is the key to connecting with others. Those who master these laws create a number of open doors in life. Combined, these two laws create the perfect stage for you to engage others and wow them with how you leave them feeling. Strong communication skills are essential on your success journey. Let's establish the three greatest determinants of your success path as it relates to the Law of Communication:

The three greatest determinants of your communication success path

1. Sustained growth and development of your communication skills

2. Sharpening your listening skills

3. The power of words

Developing strong communication skills

First, we will discuss the improvement of communication skills and how to sustain growth and continuous development. You must have the desire to communicate effectively in order to place yourself in a position of continuous development. The power of effective communication will not happen on its own and can only truly be realized to the fullest when a concerted effort to improve is made.

Sharpening your listening skills

Sharpening your listening skills will bring you more respect and interpersonal growth than just about any other endeavor. People like to feel they are being heard. When you clearly listen to others, you are honoring the power of communication by investing the time to take in their messages.

Think about this for a moment: Whenever someone acknowledges the words you have spoken, you always feel appreciated and valued. This value is proof that others were paying attention to your dialogue when they're able to reflect upon your words. A good way to see people's self-esteem rise quickly is to pay them a compliment for words well spoken. You will witness their entire body language come alive. This certainly piques their interest in you.

The power of words

The power of words cannot be overstated. There are legions of people who place no value on the words they use and the results are to their detriment. Whenever I'm involved with others who speak recklessly and without regard to the feelings of others, I find creative ways to excuse myself from their presence.

Oftentimes, offenders such as this don't even realize the

hurt and damage they leave behind in their paths. I call this a bad case of "stupid mouth" - that is, when you constantly let the misuse and abuse of your words create havoc for others, all the while escaping recognition of this. This is truly stupid, when we know a little bit of awareness and responsible use of words could right wrongful situations. There are other instances when intelligent people simply use the wrong words and the consequences are equally damaging.

We have established that a positive mental attitude is paramount for allowing our lives to be open to success. That, however, is by no means the only task involved. Strong communication skills also set the tone for success in life. All other aspects of development follow the power of diligently increasing your communication skills.

In order to improve the path of success exponentially, you must be able to connect with a number of people from varying backgrounds and learn to understand and employ the words they use. Although you will need to leave the comfort of the herd in order to get the needed variation, opening yourself up to unique personalities, different ethnic cultures, various religious perspectives and other worldly influences will allow you to expand horizons. This creates readily available avenues for success greater than you may have ever imagined. The ability to embrace the power of words and to communicate well, ties into how you leave others feeling. Interpersonal synergy, especially with mavens and connectors, opens up opportunities for communication. Furthermore, by opening yourself up, you are also allowing the diversity of the world into your life. Perhaps you will find something that you will welcome with open arms, perhaps not. But if you fail to allow the opportunity, you are minimizing your development. It is the opportunity to benefit from a range of interactions and to focus on how well you have left others feeling, that really matters.

The greater your communication skills, the more numerous the connections that are available to you will become. You'll also create more open lines of communication with these varying opportunities and global perspectives. I will explore the power of words from additional perspectives later on in this chapter.

The Law of Communication tunes into station WIIFM

The Law of Communication dictates that when you help other people achieve what they want and reach their goals, they will help you achieve what you want and realize your aspirations. We have heard countless professionals speak about the best way of doing this and the general consensus is that the very best way is to tune into everyone's favorite radio station: WIIFM - what's in it for me.

When people believe and see that they are able to gain something from interacting with you, they are far more interested in engaging with you. This creates a magnetic draw to you; people want to be around you and feel as though they are gaining strength and encouragement from you. When you help them reach their goals, they are more than willing to help you achieve yours, because they feel privileged to have the opportunity to give back to you.

As I mentioned earlier, I had this same feeling drawing me toward Whoopi Goldberg and Muhammad Ali. I learned that each of their abilities to effectively converse reflected their powerful and persuasive communication skills. It was a connection to their personal power, beyond their celebrity status.

Consider the future when you expand your reach through the Law of Communication. A dedicated effort at using this law will net you the opportunity for choice relationships and as time progresses, you'll be able to surround yourself with people who are drawn to you. Consequently, you can begin to draw strength from them. When their lives change because you elect to help them, you acquire the grand opportunity to experience positive change in your own life because you gained multiple people who may be committed to helping you. These people make awesome candidates for the mastermind concept noted earlier.

When station WIIFM turns into station WIIFY

Take a moment and realize the treasures gained as a result of building powerful communication skills. Previous to opening the lines of communication to others and offering your best assistance during the process of developing these quality relationships, your ability to receive assistance from others was most likely limited.

The key is to first become what it is you seek. In order to have a good friend, you must be a good friend. In order to receive the charity of others, you must give charity to others. This of course is the Law of Sowing and Reaping showing its hand inside the Law of Communication. Both the Law of Sowing and Reaping and the Law of Communication leave others feeling good about your personal code of conduct, your personal signature and your commitment to others.

When you help improve the outlook of others via the use of strong communication skills and by showing your value to them, people are far more likely to tune into your station, WIIFY (what's in it for you). The reason for wanting to help others must be pure and without an expectation of instant or long-term reward for your efforts. Consequently, the laws of the universe will work in your favor at another point in time, thus changing the station to WIIFY. This happens without your ever adjusting the radio dial. As you make a concerted effort to stay tuned to other people's needs, you will grasp the full meaning of the Law of Communication and learn the power of how you leave them feeling.

You must allow the Law of Communication to become part of your lifestyle. Accept and open yourself to this and your inner knowing of your interpersonal relationships will change dramatically. When working to develop the best from your relationships, remember that everyone's favorite subject is themselves. Martin Luther King said it best: "We all have the drum major instinct; we all want to be out front! We all want to lead the parade.

"We all have the drum major instinct; we all want to be out front! We all want to lead the parade"

- Martin Luther King, Jr.

When you have a real respect for the Law of Communication, you will be able to build rapport at high levels and dramatically build influence. To say that you are communicating effectively does not merely mean being able to speak; it is being able to interact with others on various levels. As you build influence in people's lives, you will know you are on the road to success and affluence. Moreover, you can enlist a call-to-action in others. Consistently following this pattern makes a powerful impression and you are able to leave people feeling good about themselves time and time again.

Navigating through mine fields

The Law of Communication recognizes that, throughout life, we gain knowledge from the challenges we face. These challenges may often feel like we are at war and face an explosion at every turn - much like crossing a minefield. Typically, when a minefield explodes, the central fireworks erupt and scatter a number of smaller fireworks that create challenges.

Successfully navigating your way through the mine fields of life requires that you effectively combat whatever problems you are faced with. You must not only learn from challenges, but also gain essential skills that enable you to avoid unnecessary trouble.

Navigating your way through the mine fields of life is not easy, nor is it supposed to be. If it were easy, we would never learn anything! Mine fields in life are those times of hardship that create explosive points that seem to blow up, scattering into a number of other problems. The true value of these circumstances is measured in how you react to these predicaments, not the predicament itself.

Additionally, mine fields in life may also come in the form of adversity or setbacks. As you press through present adversity and setbacks, you need to develop a keen sense of where future mine fields lie. This keen sense comes in the combination of both experience and intuition, which help to ring the danger alarm for similar reoccurrences.

You must use this keen sense of awareness to avoid future troubles and the sin of making the same mistakes repeatedly. Build your character from life's lessons. Let your moral fiber soar as a result of both living in the moment and developing an increasing awareness of the future. You must maintain vigilance in the midst of life's many mine fields!

As I move through my personal and professional endeavors, I feel a deep sense of responsibility. I take ownership in helping to manage the needs of my friends and clients. It is this responsibility that fuels my finest intentions as I work with each of them to help them learn how to avoid or combat potentially tragic consequences. These consequences arise from stepping onto one of life's mine fields. Although most of us learn from our past, we gain much more by understanding and using the universal laws discussed thus far. The goal is to see a potential minefield and have the life skills to disarm the situation before you jeopardize your position.

Discovering alternative approaches for managing obstacles

Alternative approaches for managing challenges may be discovered in the obstacles themselves. You must take life's obstacles and use them to your advantage. Whether it is a major annoyance, such as a minefield, or something smaller, such as a firecracker, you must be able to attack these obstacles with pinpoint accuracy.

I find the very best way of making an obstacle work in my favor is by looking to create a symbiotic relationship anytime I can: in other words, a mutually beneficial relationship. There will be times when this tactic will not be applicable. But whenever you can apply this tactic, you will reduce your stress and increase your odds of progress, regardless of the ensuing trouble. In nature, there is strong evidence that animals create symbiotic relationships with their environment and predators.

One clear example of a symbiotic relationship is that of the sea anemone. Sea anemones look like beautiful flowers. The most common varieties are deep red, purple and pink, with black centers. These invertebrates live attached to the sea floor, rock or coral. They have also been known to attach themselves to hermit crabs. Sea anemones are long lived; this brightly colored creature doesn't worry much about being eaten, because it is loaded with powerful poisonous stingers, called nematocysts. Some fish that share the anemone's environment have a protective mucous coating which keeps them from being injured by the anemone. But other fish can be killed by the anemone's stinging tentacles. The anemone protects some species of fish, while these, in turn, lure different fish to the anemone for food. This is an example of symbiosis, another common adaptation for survival.

The additional symbiotic relationship is the taxi service provided by the hermit crab. The hermit crab chauffeurs the sea anemone around while navigating under the protection of those powerful stinging cells that attract perpetual food to both hermit crab and sea anemone. It is profitable for both parties. Many dangers of the sea have been neutralized by these symbiotic relationships. This collaborative relationship is a prime example of a "host-beneficiary relationship," a symbiotic relationship! It is no accident that sea anemones have long lives, as they ward off predators via the process of symbiosis.

Think of the situations and relationships in your life where you might disarm the mine fields by following the lead of the hermit crab and the sea anemone. How many times could you have improved your lifestyle by creating a symbiotic or host-beneficiary relationship with the obstacles that come into your world? Do you recall that old adage that says, "Keep your friends close and your enemies closer?" The operative word here is closer. Could there be more loaded in that old saying than merely the words? And can you see that the most powerful examples of symbiotic relationships require that the participants connect very closely?

The message is profound. The strongest survive because they learn how to adapt and adjust in a "dog-eat-dog" environment - and they live longer! A key benefit to symbiotic relationships is that they allow you to move forward without having to watch your every step. You might say the more of these relationships that you can form in life, the more people you have watching your back. How would that notion leave you feeling?

You might be inclined to think that the symbiotic relationships that help you navigate through the mine fields of life are often acquired by mere chance. There will be times in your life when you will find you have been given a break and you may consider yourself lucky. But I don't believe that luck simply befalls us. Luck is drawn from the number of actions and endeavors at which you persist.

Luck is nothing more than your preparedness coinciding with the opportunities in life. For a more in-depth perspective regarding luck, I recommend an interesting book called "The Luck Factor", by Dr. Richard Wiseman. Wiseman profiles the essential principles for creating more luck in your life from a scientific perspective.

After three years of intensive interviews and experiments with more than 400 volunteers, Wiseman arrived at an astonishing conclusion: Luck is something that can be learned. It is available to anyone willing to pay attention to the Four Essential Principles: creating chance opportunities, thinking lucky, feeling lucky and denying fate.

If life has not stopped hammering on you, I encourage you to prepare in the following way as you navigate through its troubles and challenges. Discover ways of increasing your luck. Where and when needed, seek the best tools for creating symbiotic relationships. Never lose your forward momentum and strive to discover your life's calling.

"Even if you're on the right track, you'll get run over if you just sit there."

- Will Rogers

The more focused you are, the easier it gets for you to find clear paths through the mine fields. Remember, being in the right place at the right time and being ready are not enough to ensure success - you must also keep moving forward. As Will Rogers states, "Even if you're on the right track, you'll get run over if you just sit there."

Being lucky and taking full advantage of life's gifts are what dreams are made of. Daring to push your imagination and discover your passion and purpose is the recipe for a fulfilling lifestyle. One has to truly connect with this point to fully embrace it and understand this blissful place in life. As Henry David Thoreau expressed it, "If one advances confidently in the direction of his dreams and endeavors to live the life which he has imagined, he will meet with success unexpected in common hours."

Fine-tuning your tone

You can further reduce the obstacles in your life by fine-tuning your tone for greater effectiveness. Two integral parts of the Law of Communication are what you say and how you say it. Too many times, people will say something and the intended meaning is received in a totally different manner. You must pay close attention to the inflection in your voice, which is often referred to as your tone of voice.

You need to ensure that your delivery matches your intention. Monitoring the manner of your interpersonal communication will enhance the image you want to portray with others. These good perceptions that others have of how you communicate will improve your relationships. Your tone of speech can in many ways set the tone and height of your personal and professional growth. I have heard it said, "Your wallet is a direct reflection of the extent of your vocabulary."

When talking with people, we are sometimes unaware of the subtle tones or inadvertent hints we give off. The key is to learn to develop your communication skills so people will want to hear whatever you have to say. Thus, they will want to be near you as well. The big questions you may be asking yourself are: How do I work on my communication skills? And how do I know if I have the right or wrong tone? Well, we all communicate on various levels: our body language, facial expressions, hand gestures and tone. The following scenario will help you work on these various facets of your communication skills.

A colleague of yours is working on a new project in the

"If one advances confidently in the direction of his dreams and endeavors to live the life which he has imagined, he will meet with success unexpected in common hours."

- Henry David Thoreau

office. A little unsure of himself, he keeps coming to you with questions. As the day progresses, you are getting tired of him always running in and asking what you may consider "dumb" questions.

Keep in mind: to him they are not dumb questions. After the 10th or 15th question, you are ready to say, "Get out of here, go ask someone else!" Even though you want to say it, you may not. But your tone is clear - you are frustrated with him. Perhaps the next time he comes into your office, you could invite him in, sit him down and ask if there is something else bothering him that you may be able to help with. You are far more inviting and you have made him feel important. This will give you the opportunity to suggest a different course of action and your impact on this individual will be far greater than before.

Finding a way to make a positive impact in someone's life will help you develop the necessary skills to increase the success of your life's journey. The example above can work in many areas. The lesson is not exactly new - think before you speak - but the Law of Communication is much more than that. Speak with intent and sincerity, because when you do, people will be drawn to your message and these people will ultimately aid in your success, while you, in turn, help them to achieve their own personal and professional success.

"It takes a lifetime to build credibility and an instant to destroy it."

- Unknown

You must remain honorable to your words; if you tell someone you are going to do something, anything short of following through is not an option. I encourage you to speak with sincerity and do not promise something you can't and don't fully intend to deliver. The people to whom you make promises will remember them, even if you forget. When you do not follow through on your commitments, people begin to distrust you. When you lose a person's trust, it is very difficult to recapture it. Your credibility is only as good as your last broken promise. I have heard it said, "It takes a lifetime to build credibility and an instant to destroy it."

Earning integrity through the power of your words

Lasting success can never be attained when there is a question regarding your integrity. I have an aunt who promised me long ago that if I could make it through college and graduate, she would give me a special vacation as a reward. She pledged to take me to Jamaica if I was the first in my family to graduate from college. It has been twenty-one years since I graduated from college. She did not keep her promise.

After all these years, I still remember that one broken promise and find myself telling the story when I want to drive home the message about doing what you say you are going to do. This builds integrity. Conversely, neglecting to do what you say you are going to do demonstrates your lack of integrity and people are slow to forget it.

Speaking with truth and sincerity is important, but you must also be mindful of the context of what you say. Many people are quoted by the news media and look back and try to explain what they actually meant. But now, after the fact, it is too late.

With respect to the Law of Communication, the tone and content of what you say are equally important. Words are extremely powerful. The Law of Communication states that your thoughts and actions become your reality. The cosmos is listening. Can you recall a time when something spectacular had come into your world and your immediate reaction was this is unbelievable? The real intention of your response is to communicate your gratification at the situation and thus a more appropriate phrase with which to respond would be, this is awesome! To respond by using the word unbelievable is actually negative and denotes your disbelief in the fortune. There should be no disbelief, as the evidence of the fortune is in fact what you are responding to.

Conversely, by using the word awesome, you convey the response of how grand the fortune is and this opens the door for more awesome experiences to come into your life. Although the word unbelievable may sometimes have similar meanings to the word awesome, it also conveys that you can't totally take in what has happened. And this connotation could be perceived by the subconscious mind as negative thinking. Believing awesome things are destined to come into your life is kin to subscribing to positive affirmations. Let me share a personal story that illustrates the power of words.

The cosmos is listening to your words

A few years ago, I was working as a casino marketing executive at the Bellagio Casino and Resort in Las Vegas, Nevada. My wife, Teresa and I were having a conversation about some woman at her workplace who constantly questioned her about how I was doing at the Bellagio. I didn't know this woman and, other than seeing her in the hallway or locker room, neither did Teresa.

My wife is a very private person and she did not welcome the interrogation. She really didn't know how to answer the questions. In her frustration and attempts at trying to get the woman off her back, she blurted out, "My husband has been terminated from Bellagio!" Teresa was telling me the story while I was getting dressed to head off to work at the Bellagio. I responded to her by saying that she should be very careful of her words: "The universe is listening - words are very powerful!"

I pointed out that when someone asks a personal question, rather than making up something far-fetched just to get rid of him or her, simply say, "Well, that is an interesting question, why do you ask?" This way, you avoid carelessly choosing words that shape negative possibilities.

When I returned from work that evening, I met my wife in the driveway and warmly greeted her as she emerged from her car. We exchanged brief pleasantries. I then said calmly, "I got terminated today." She said, "No you didn't." I replied, "Yes, I really did." My wife's first words after understanding that this was no joke were: "Oh my God! I said that very thing this morning!"

This clearly demonstrates how words, however insignificant you may think they are at the time, can impact critical situations. You should consider how you could use the Law of Communication to your advantage. Imagine how you can become a far more dynamic person by observing and respecting the Law of Communication. Use the power of words to leave others - and yourself - feeling good!

Positive self-talk strengthens your self-esteem

How would you take the initial step in strengthening your self-esteem? Use positive words when thinking or talking about yourself. Your first step in the direction of using positive words must be to ask yourself the following: "What actions can I take immediately to improve myself in this area?" Many times, it is to simply become aware of your self-talk.

The request I made of you in prior sections to be mindful of your words is not limited to the words you use when speaking to others. It also applies to the words you use with yourself. This is your mind's self-talk or brain chatter. For instance, if you have been a blue-collar worker for much of your life and find yourself in a white-collar work situation, you may maintain blue-collar mentality. How you see yourself depends on your familiar paradigm. You will have a blue-collar mentality struggling to function in a white-collar world. This is not a comfortable or productive fit.

With this type of thinking, words can be used in a negative fashion. Although you aspire to a higher level, you refuse to change core beliefs about who you really are. It becomes self-limiting and de-motivating to place labels and titles on one another and on ourselves. In order for you to grow into an evolved being from the inside out, your self-talk must match the language that you use when speaking to others. The world can see it when you are living a life in which your inner world is not a reflection of your outer world - that is, when your life's message is inconsistent with your being. Start by using positive words to describe yourself; use mantras and affirmations to clear your head of negative self-talk.

You may have had an upbringing that was incorrectly slanted by people creating challenging life conditions for you - even though they were probably using the only skills they knew to shape a young mind. Rather than growing up with strong self-esteem from constantly being told that you could be anyone you wanted to be, you may have received negative reinforcement from parents or influential adults in your life.

In other words, a poor self-image doesn't start with self. It often starts with what others have hammered into your head. Generally, the words that you use to describe yourself come from the words that have been forced onto you from early in your life.

If you are fortunate enough to have a positive self-image, it is most likely because your early influence was positive and you learned how to better value and evaluate your place in this world. Your value system and self-esteem are fundamental to how you develop a positive voice and how you maintain that voice through the selection of words that you use with both self and others.

When I recommend being mindful of the Law of Communication, I am not suggesting a complete change in how you speak with others. Simply monitor your dialogue and make small enhancements as needed. At the end of the day, you will receive your largest improvements from the combined effects of smaller improvements. It's the small changes in people that have the greatest impact. A lasting way to experience sustained growth is by positive internalization.

Can you recall a time when the game was on the line and a series of heated positive affirmations helped put you or your team on the winning side? There is a momentum shift that occurs whenever positive vibrations are felt and it is that shift that usually triumphs in the end. "It is not the mountain that we conquer, but ourselves," as Edmund Hillary said.

I recently played in an international volleyball game in which two companies were pitted against one another. This was an annual match and we were playing in the Dominican Republic at the beautiful Sun Village Beach Resort, located in Puerto Plata. The trophy, plus $500 to the EMI Foundation, were on the line. The game was coming down to the wire with only a few points separating either team from victory. Emotions were running high and both sides wanted to win. The teams were equally matched and the momentum had shifted back and forth several times throughout the contest.

I was playing for the Sun Village Beach Resort, against an international company, Impact Net Worth, headquartered in Las Vegas, Nevada. The momentum in the final stretch was clearly on their side. I called a strategic time-out and ran over to the trophy podium. I snatched the trophy from the stand, aggressively planting it in the sand on our side of the net. I put the volleyball in

"It is not the mountain that we conquer, but ourselves."

- Edmund Hillary

the trophy. I shouted to our team, "Whose trophy is this? Whose trophy is this?! How bad do you want to win this trophy? How bad do you want this trophy?!" The team responded in a loud and positive roar: "That trophy is ours; we are going to win this!"

I looked across the net at our worthy opponents. I could see the energy loss and the momentum shift for the final winning points. We won the game and I believe the last minute push of positive words and affirmations is what propelled us to victory. Words are very powerful and they exert their force even when you don't know they are doing so.

By being aware of the Law of Communication, you become more aware of how the world hears you and how you hear yourself. As you learn to control your internal and external communication, you will find greater success. Your destiny will be shaped by your ability to firmly and consistently execute the Law of Communication.

The Law of Communication - a symbolic pipeline

"You will be the same person you are now ten years from now, except for the people that you meet and the books that you read and how you manage your own life experiences."

- Charlie Temendous Jones and Jesse Ferrell

The Law of Communication and the Law of Attitude create a dynamic duo when working in unison. They will consistently impact one another and are often present at the same time. Your willingness to harness and utilize the Law of Communication will be the key that opens the treasure trove of life's many gifts. The principal of these gifts will come in the form of people that you meet on your journey. Charlie Tremendous Jones said, "You will be the same person you are now ten years from now, except for the people that you meet and the books that you read." To this quote I have added an important jewel, which is the third communication key to opening life's treasure trove. It is: "and how you manage your own life experiences." This powerful statement is well supported by the Law of Communication. The Law of Attitude is the gateway to the Law of Communication. If you cannot develop a positive attitude, your route to consistent and effective communication will be blocked. Think of it this way: the Law of Communication is the pipeline and the Law of Attitude opens the way to it, together allowing the free flow of your thoughts and words. Most people refuse to engage with, or to assist, those who have a toxic attitude, because they can't stand being around them. Your chief reasons for desiring to communicate effectively should be to understand the needs and desires of others and to help others understand your primary concerns.

As you work to build a variety of relationships, the power of communication becomes essential to your success and provides the lift to the top of the mountain. Conversely, a lack of clear communication erects walls of discontent. These walls of discontent become barriers to truth and the side effects can be fear, resentment, turmoil, confusion, distrust and deceit. These all result from and perpetuate, communication breakdowns.

At the end of the day, your desire to become an effective communicator is your ticket to engaging in the power of how you leave them feeling via the Law of Communication. The how you leave them feeling concept is what moves others and they in turn move you! Your unwillingness to respect and submit to these principles will result in countless lost opportunities for growth and prosperity. Communication skills will take you farther down the path of success than any other aspect of good relationships.

Those of us who are full of enthusiasm and unafraid to express it, often run across the problem of interrupting others when they are speaking or finishing their sentences. Enthusiasm is good, but must be controlled to the degree that you refrain from interrupting others or finishing their sentences. Even if you are certain of what the other speaker is going to say, allow them to finish their sentence whenever they have the floor. This is a positive sign of validation and people love to have their thoughts and words validated. This is important for upholding their self-esteem and plays right into the how you leave them feeling message.

Use your sense of timing to know when to exit a conversation with others and never overstay your welcome. It is prudent to observe that you cannot always say exactly what you are thinking. Never use a 100 dollar word if a nickel word will do. Don't speak to impress; speak to express! Your face must express the interest you have in others. If your words are telling a different story than the expressions you wear on your face, others will believe your expressions and body language rather than your words.

Always make and maintain respectful eye contact, without staring at others. You will experience a natural high when you have communicated effectively with others. On the other hand, poor communication skills will cost you dearly. They are most often the dreaded killer of many failing relationships. You might also think of poor communication skills as the silent killer of prosperity. Most people think the breakdown is not their fault, even though their inability to prosper is evident. Such people often perceive the fault to be the other person's and generally take no responsibility for the ineffective communication. From that perspective, there can be no measure of corrective behavior. Repairing the damage of misunderstanding thus becomes a lost possibility.

Three critical points of the Law of Communication

To help you avoid an irreparable breakdown in communication and the kind of unrewarding situation to which it leads, I have identified three critical points of the Law of Communication. In all your encounters, be aware of:

1. The power of clarity and focus
2. The power of intention
3. The tone of your words

The power of clarity

The power of clarity and focus is the major force in advancing our communication skills. Whenever we are clear on what it is we want, we need to focus our delivery so that the message hits its target. The desire for mutual understanding with others represents the initial fuel needed to power the engine of communication. It is this desire that compels us to resolve complex issues and that brings about closure to a myriad of concerns.

The power of intention

The second point of communication concerns our intention. Closely examining our feelings, while focusing on our desire to communicate effectively, directs us to match intention with the action taken. The end goal is to strengthen the quality of communication. A checkup from the neck up in monitoring our intentions brings power to the Law of Communication.

The tone of your words

The tone that others use to communicate with us will serve to pique our interest and encourage us to play a willing role in advancing communications. It can also turn us off, should we feel the slightest bit of condescension or judgment. Conversely, we must keep our own tone in check as we reach out to others. Oftentimes, it is the quality of your tone that causes a breakdown in communication, rather than the content of your dialogue. I firmly believe you can say nearly anything you want to others, as long as you remain respectful and choose the right tone of delivery. Adopting just the right tone heightens the value of your message.

"They don't care how much you know, until they know how much you care."

- Unknown

People determine how they feel about you by your kindness and tone of voice. Have you ever become instantly irritated with someone by listening to their tone of speech, even though you may not be able to hear or understand their words? If their tone of speaking is irritating, it raises your blood pressure immediately and you don't care what they have to say from that point forward. I'm reminded of a quote by an unknown author, which says, "They don't care how much you know, until they know how much you care." The truth of this quote rings loudly: We tend to care more about what others have to say when we know how much they care about us.

Although it is important to be good to others, is there such a thing as being too good to someone? I think you can recall a time in which you may have been too good to someone. Whenever you find yourself in a relationship where you're the one who is burdened with turning a negative interaction into something amicable, it becomes very mentally exhausting.

Do you find that you are the one who apologizes in order to reduce the tension of a bad bout of communication? If you are the pleaser in your relationship, the weight of correction will find itself in your lap. You may have the "disease to please," whereby you work very hard to please everyone around you. I discovered a very good book called "The Disease to Please", by Harriet B. Braiker, Ph.D. People who fall into this category are strong candidates for those who may fit the role of being too good to others while causing mental strain to themselves.

You can avoid the worst of the disease to please if you simply revisit some of the values of communication described above. You can thus discover clues as to how others want to be treated. Such clues are typically written all over their faces. You can observe their attention span, eye contact, expressions, body language, ability to focus on your conversation and many other signs. All of these clues scream the message of how they want to be treated and you have the responsibility of honoring their request. You can politely help them understand that you will treat them respectfully and in the manner they are requesting whenever they earn or live up to the desired respect. This is different from reflexively and unthinkingly trying to please.

The information above illustrates how to treat others by carefully observing their expressions and it delivers valuable insight. The book "Blink", by Malcolm Gladwell, tells the story of how we react to certain expressions and notes that human beings are capable of delivering a combination of 6,000 expressions. Gladwell shares a tragic story of how officers opened fire on an innocent victim after misreading the facial expression, intention and actions of a man who was innocently sitting on his own porch. Although this is a dramatic case, it conveys the power of facial expressions and the need to use them to accurately interpret the intentions of others. Expressions play a major role in the communication cycle.

Joni and the gift of a smile

Though we have discussed many elements of improving your attitude and avenues of communication, there remains one significant element that we have not discussed. It is simple and easy to perform and anyone can do it. It is the power of a smile! A smile is infectious and has been scientifically proven to make us feel better whenever we employ it. There are many ways of delivering a smile. To name a few, you can smile in person, smile over the phone or send a smile through the mail.

A few years ago, I sent a smile through the mail to a good friend by the name of Joni Pippa. In this smile package, Joni received a short letter of appreciation recognizing our friendship in a small red envelope. The red envelope had gold Chinese characters printed on the outside, which symbolized faith and good fortune. Joni had been recently released from her job and was told that the commissions she had earned up to the point of termination were going to be forfeited as per their standard company policy. This misfortune would make Joni late on her rent, utilities and other pending responsibilities. Unfortunately, she was without a penny of savings in the bank to catch this fall.

Of the several communications Joni received in the mail that day, she chose to read my letter first. After reading it, she proceeded to open the red envelope, which included a two-dollar bill that I loaded with the blind intention of enlisting good fortune to come her way. I had not been aware of Joni's situation before developing the idea to send fortune her way.

Between my letter and small gesture of good fortune, Joni was overwhelmed with positive feelings and found herself smiling. She then opened the next envelope, which was from her former employer. Her former employer had reversed the policy of releasing commissions to terminated employees and sent her a check for nearly one thousand dollars. Joni credits the good karma of the smile package that I sent to the receipt of the one thousand dollars from her former employer. After sharing her feelings with me during a telephone conversation, she then sent me the following passage regarding the cost of a smile. I share it with you as I have for appropriate audiences during my professional speaking endeavors:

A Smile Costs Nothing and Gives Much

A smile costs nothing and gives much. It enriches those who receive, without making poorer those who give. It takes but a moment, but the memory of it can sometimes last forever.

None is so rich or mighty that he can get along without it and none is so poor but that he can be made rich by it. A smile creates happiness in the home, fosters good will in business and it's the countersign of friendship.

It brings rest to the weary, cheer to the discouraged and sunshine to the sad. It is nature's best antidote for trouble, yet it cannot be begged, borrowed, or stolen, for it is of no value to anyone, unless it is given away. Some people are too tired to give you a smile. Give them one of yours, as none needs a smile so much as he who has no more to give.

- Author Unknown

Key Action Steps
The Law of Communication

Action Step 1
Tune into everyone's favorite radio station - WIIFM

The first step in tuning into anyone's favorite radio station is to remain open to receiving its signal. Make a concerted effort to determine what others want from you by using all of your senses. Oftentimes, others will send you nonverbal clues as to what their needs are and you must be vigilant in recognizing and receiving those clues. After interpreting the clues, take every possible avenue toward honoring their requests. When working in this diligent and perceptive fashion, you will earn bonus points toward the quality of your relationships. Demonstrate your ability for tuning into everyone's favorite radio station, WIIFM. This puts you in a class of few, because many people simply will not take the time to do this. This method of communication always leaves others feeling good!

Action Step 2
Navigate through the mine fields of life

"In the long run, men hit only what they aim at."

- Henry David Thoreau

There will always be problems to solve, conflict resolution and crisis management in our lives. Any one of these challenging situations can turn into a full-blown minefield! The true essence of life is about how you manage these predicaments. The best way to navigate through the mine fields of life is by confronting these annoyances head-on. Move with a sense of urgency toward solutions. Regardless of the severity of the challenge, you must take aim toward swift correction and resolution, which are your key targets. Henry David Thoreau has this to say about targets: "In the long run, men hit only what they aim at." Have you heard of the saying, "Don't make a mountain out of a molehill?" My experience prompts me to direct you to interpret this saying differently. Best practices suggest stomping out even the molehills, because they eventually mushroom into Mount Everest "want-to-be's!"

A major mistake I see quite often is when people neglect to take action to resolve their challenges. There are two approaches that are prevalent: ignoring the problem and hoping it resolves itself, or focusing all energy on the problem itself. Neither of these approaches will bring you consistently positive results. After discovering a problem, all of your energies must be aimed at creating options for resolution. This single concept is the best action step to leave both yourself and others feeling good.

Action Step 3
Create a symbiotic relationship with obstacles in life

Whenever I'm engaged in a coaching session with clients and we are working through their life plans, the discussion of dreams and goals creates a breakthrough for them. Most people have dreams, yet few people have written goals and an established life plan. In order to best facilitate the process of establishing goals and a life plan, I create a customized JessTalk Lifestyles Portfolio for all of my Lifestyles clients. The JessTalk Lifestyles Portfolio is a plan that addresses every key point of personal and professional development for the client. It starts with the client's life vision and moves backwards through a 90-day plan with specific action steps.

The most common problems occur when people are either at a crossroads in their lives or they have run into obstacles. Rather than letting those obstacles impede their progress, I recommend creating a symbiotic relationship. This is similar to that of the sea anemone and the hermit crab. This method allows others to help themselves and their situation, while reveling in the fact that what was once an obstacle has been turned into something mutually beneficial.

Action Step 4
Let the power of words shape your life

If we are only to take one lesson from this chapter it is: "the cosmos is listening." This should positively alter the words you use. Many of us were taught to deal with people who said mean things to us by reciting an old nursery rhyme. The rhyme said, "Sticks and stones may break my bones, but words will never hurt me." The trick was that if you said this rhyme following something hurtful, like name-calling that was directed at you, it would make things better. I disagreed with this old wives' tale as a child and, to this day, I still don't believe it works.

Words are powerful and when we use them as a weapon, they can cut like a knife. You may not draw blood by using negative or harsh words with others, but you can do permanent internal damage. I have heard my share of stories in which people have reached ages beyond their mid-forties and are still affected by the harsh words used by their parents. Using truthful and powerful words can have the opposite effect. Whenever I point out the positive and truthful characteristics to my clients, it lifts their spirits and boosts their self-esteem. "Words can sometimes, in moments of grace, attain the quality of deeds," states Elie Wiesel, author and activist. Choose your words carefully; you may be shaping someone's life!

Action Step 5
Strengthen your self-esteem with positive self-talk

Take every opportunity to strengthen your self-esteem by using positive self-talk. Read daily affirmations, listen to guided positive meditation programs and create a list of positive motivations for accomplishing your desired goals. Read it audibly on a daily basis. Surround yourself with people who help you improve yourself and who boost your self-esteem. Refuse to spend time with people who either bring you down or cause your energy levels to dip.

Take time out for yourself; work in some decompression time in which you do absolutely nothing. Allow yourself the gift of enjoying the human experience by actually becoming a human being, rather than a human doing. The exercise of doing absolutely nothing is quite refreshing. Give yourself a chance to decompress and erase outdated mental programming.

Unplug from the mechanical and high-tech information age for blocks of time. No cell phones, land lines, televisions, internet, beepers, radios or stereos. Call a time-out from this information-age superhighway. Reconnect with nature. Seek the calm of lakes, oceans, trees, mountains and fresh air! This will help to restore your pure thoughts and allow you the opportunity to complete a full cleanse - a checkup from the neck up. Connect with your passion and spend time holding your vision. I always believe, "If I can touch it and see it, I can do it and be it!" Whenever you return from this well-earned time-out, remember to bring your refreshed attitude with you. Yes, you can do it!

"If I can touch it and see it, I can do it and be it!"

- Jesse Ferrell

Summary Points
The Second Essential Law of Life
The Law of Communication

1. Continuously develop your communication skills; sharpen your listening skills and embrace the power of words

2. Allow your experience and intuition to help you navigate through the mine fields of life

3. Build your character through the muscle of capturing life's many lessons

4. Make tough obstacles part of your plan by creating symbiotic relationships with them

5. Be mindful of the words you use with yourself - maintain positive self-talk

6. Don't speak to impress; speak to express

7. Tune into everyone's favorite radio station: WIIFM

Affirmations
Moments for Reflection

1. I always listen intently to others and determine what their needs are

2. I embrace life's challenges while focusing on solutions

3. I find every avenue possible to make problem solving a personal strength

4. I fully understand the power of words and choose my words carefully

5. My inner voice remains steadfast toward creating a life of abundance

Chapter 5

The Best Way to Leave People Feeling

In this chapter, you will learn seven key ways to leave people feeling good. As you practice the seven keys listed below, you will notice your interpersonal relationships improving. The benefit of improved relationships is the tip of the iceberg in terms of personal and professional growth. I have found sustained success by using these seven key ways to leave others feeling good. And I'm certain these fundamental keys will either serve as a foundation or reaffirmation for you.

Seven key ways to leave others feeling good

1. Learn from others and welcome the universal law of giving

2. Leave others wanting more

3. Leave an impression on others that they matter

4. Learn their name and use it during conversation

5. Apologize at the appropriate times

6. Learn to listen well and make eye contact during conversation

7. Maintain a responsible, balanced attitude

First key way to leave others feeling good: learn from others

I love learning from other people and whenever I'm given the opportunity to do so, I take it. Whenever you allow the learning process to take place by becoming teachable, you welcome the universal law of giving and always make others feel good. It rewards them with the joy of helping you. As I perform my responsibilities of helping others through my life coaching practice, I'm reminded, on a daily basis, how nice it feels to help others move forward in their lives.

The bigger the challenge I'm able to help my clients discover solutions for, the better I feel about the help I'm giving them. You don't have to be a life coach to offer others help and feel the same personal gratification that I do.

Second key way to leave others feeling good: leave them wanting more

The best way to leave people feeling good is to leave them wanting more. If you are a professional speaker, all of your performances should be geared toward leaving people wanting to hear more from you. Studies have proven that people generally remember the first and last things they either read or hear. With this in mind, it is prudent to load your most important material in a manner that your audiences will be able to recall. That is, convey messages they can use following your speaking performance.

If you are a performer, challenge yourself to do every performance as though it is your last. Put your heart and soul into each opportunity. Your audience will feel your energy and be uplifted by your efforts. They will be left wanting more, because we can all use such energy boosts.

Third key way to leave others feeling good: leave an impression on others that they matter

People like to know that they matter to you. Learn to remember the names of people you meet. Use their names frequently during conversation. The sound of hearing your own name is worth more than gold to most of us. Whenever you encounter someone you have met in the past, never launch into that tired old routine of "I never forget a face; I know your face, but I just can't remember your name." What in the world does that trite expression mean anyway? How can you know a face? You would do much better by greeting them with sincerity and simply saying: "Hello my name is Allen. I'm sorry, I remember meeting you last month, but for the life of me, I can't recall your name. Please do me the favor of telling me again."

Most people will value your honesty. This also gives you another chance to hear their name and use it while they are in your presence. This is much better than playing the pretend game of "I know your face, but I can't remember your name."

People like to feel that their thoughts, opinions and concerns are being respected. This includes giving people attention to ensure that you honor their concerns. You can bring true value to your interpersonal relationships by consistently demonstrating your desire to help others. After determining what others need, a key tactic, which will serve you well, is to simply help others before being asked. That is, rather than withholding something you know others want or need, deliver it. I have found this tactic to be fun; it is exciting to see happy expressions when I show the value of giving by remembering what is important to others. This should occur without your having to be constantly asked or reminded.

Wouldn't it feel great if you saddled up to your favorite Starbucks coffee counter and a nice server said, "Mr. Jones would you like your usual double latte with a sprinkle of cinnamon?" If you responded like most of us would, you would have a feeling of importance. Although it is only a cup of java, the fact that someone remembered your name and order, will likely keep you coming back - even during times when you are not in the mood for java. You will return for the pleasantries and the good feelings generated because someone was willing to anticipate your needs.

Fourth key way to leave others feeling good: learn their names and use them during conversation

Have you ever been involved in a conversation with someone and heard your name being spoken in another conversation within earshot? If you are like most of us, you find it difficult to concentrate on the conversation you are in. This is because the sound of your own name stimulates you to the degree that this is what you focus on. Your listening skills move to red alert. Whether it's positive or negative, you're captivated with hearing what is being spoken about you.

This scenario contains a lesson about how we should speak face-to-face with another person. A very good way to leave someone feeling good is to use their name generously throughout the conversation and, especially, as you open or close your discussion. Our own name is among the most powerful and riveting words in our personal vocabulary.

Fifth key way to leave others feeling good: apologize at the appropriate times

A well-timed apology can turn around a bad situation in a hurry. None of us are beyond making mistakes. However, the challenge after making a mistake becomes how to execute the swiftest damage control measures following the blunder. Start your damage control with two key words expressed sincerely: "I'm sorry." Those two words hold enormous healing power. Tone counts for a lot as well. As the Law of Communication says, tone is everything. If the offended person understands that you meant no intentional harm and your apology is genuine, he or she will most likely accept your apology and forgive you.

The tone of your apology will directly affect the speed of the damage control. A positive sincere tone in your delivery will most likely result in a turnaround of the offense. An insincere or apathetic apology will quite likely signal your lack of true remorse. But I have seen a simple, honest utterance of "I'm sorry" instantly transform bad situations into good.

I can attest to times when my clients have come to me with situations of conflict - between bosses, subordinates and significant others - whereby all parties were frustrated and angry with one another because of simple communication mistakes. These parties found themselves in situations where a small incident had spiraled out of control and the conflict created an impasse. What had been created was a wall of resentment. Resentment will never be helpful in your interpersonal relationships. As Carrie Fisher reminds us, "Nursing resentment is like drinking poison and waiting for the other guy to die."

"Nursing resentment is like drinking poison and waiting for the other guy to die."

- Carrie Fisher

The most common recommendation I give to clients in conflict is to take responsibility for correcting an impasse, regardless of who is right or wrong. I advise clients to look for the best time to face those offended, then offer a sincere apology and a promise to refrain from any offensive behavior in the future. In almost every case, this tactic of damage control has cleared the air for a renewed beginning and left the offended person feeling good.

There may be some unique times when you find yourself doing damage control because of a mistake made by someone else: a loved one, relative, coworker or even a boss. These cases often feel a little more precarious since you are attempting to make amends for something you didn't do.

The art of sincerity is slippery in cases such as these. I find the best way to handle things is to take ownership of the problem, express a sincere apology that the situation occurred and move directly to the fix. Determine the quickest and most responsible measure for backing up your apology with something that benefits the person who was offended. With this tactic you can take a negative situation and create an opportunity to make a friend or client for life. Just consider how the other person feels about the individual who offended them; most likely they're upset - at the very least.

Fortunately or unfortunately, you are playing the role of problem solver. Consider how the offended person may feel about you. You become the fixer, the healer of the open wound - the person giving something to the friend or client to restore their sense of self. Effectively closing that wound becomes "a feather in your cap" and the offended party will credit you with that gain.

Sense of self is usually what is destroyed when we feel disparaged by others. You can take this golden opportunity of becoming the hero. My very best and closest clients have come to me as a result of my quest to clean up a situation using precise damage control measures to right a wrong and thus effectively closing an open wound.

A twist to the story of Charles and Norma Meeks offers a case in point. Prior to meeting me, the couple had revisited a special marketing and customer service area of Bellagio on several occasions and the other executives didn't pay them the respect they deserved. The Meeks' continued to check back in this same area to see if there would be either a changing of attitudes or a changing of the guard. I happened to represent a changing of the guard, as I was on duty the fifth time they returned to get help.

After hearing their story of not receiving the appropriate customer service from our marketing team, I was eager to initiate reparation for their troubles. I took the opportunity to leave the Meeks' feeling good. As I mentioned earlier, this opportunity turned into multiple relationships full of reward for me, both personally and professionally. The unfortunate incident was transformed into a very positive succession of experiences for both the Meeks and Ferrell families. Rather than being put off by having to handle a mess created by someone else, I encourage you to see how you can transform the neglect of others into a gainful situation for all parties. The main objective is to take ownership of the problem. Take swift action to do what you can to correct the situation and leave them feeling good about the matter.

The power of words is often dramatically misunderstood as a tool for creating abundance. Whenever you use words, you create vibrations that go out into the universe and these vibrations make connections that are far reaching. They set off a chain reaction of events merely by their utterance.

Negative words create harmful vibrations that manifest into detrimental results. And positive words create positive vibrations, consequently producing desirable results. You will actually feel your energy draining when you use negative expressions regarding yourself or your life. The opposite is true when you use positive words. These positive references become energizing and uplifting.

Try this experiment. Place your hand one inch away from your mouth and start speaking into your hand. You will feel the vibration of sound bouncing back at your face as a result of the block you have placed in front of you. These vibrations normally travel out into space because there isn't a barrier to catch them. Most of us don't go around talking into our hands. Thus, without trying this experiment, you may not have realized just how much power and vibration the spoken word creates. My final caution is for you to be careful of what you say and to choose your words wisely.

Sixth key way to leave others feeling good: listen well and make eye contact during conversation

Learning to listen well can bring you continued success. You might think of listening as a lost art. Most people are more concerned with what they have to say during a conversation, rather than what the speaker is saying. Whenever you are busy thinking about what you are going to say, you can't be listening very well. Most people who employ this type of one-way communication have a bad habit of cutting other people off before they have made their point. You will not win or influence too many friends or people with a manner such as this.

Listening well and making eye contact with the person you are communicating with is a very positive step. It isn't polite or necessary to stare, but eye contact with occasional glimpses away is comforting. Making good eye contact is also a clear signal to the speaker that you are, more than likely, interested, listening attentively and taking in the message. As simple as this concept sounds, many people neglect to practice this during basic conversation. Another sure way to prove your listening skills is to periodically check for understanding by paraphrasing parts of what the speaker has said. When you recognize others properly and invest the time in listening to their point of view, you will always leave them feeling good.

Seventh key way to leave others feeling good: maintain a responsible and balanced attitude

Not so coincidentally, the seventh way to leave others feeling good is to maintain a responsible and balanced attitude. In order to maintain such an attitude, you must practice all of the aforementioned six ways to leave others feeling good. You will be handsomely rewarded if you remain flexible, rather than rigid, in your attitude. Whenever others believe you are willing to entertain options, ideas or concepts other than your own, they will be more likely to welcome you into their circle of influence. You become privy to their open communication network. This invitation into an open communication network will always lead to advanced opportunities.

The best opportunities advertised in newspapers or inner company postings are not available to most job seekers. This is because by the time of posting, the position has already been awarded to someone else. Such opportunities come to those in a network. Those of us who understand and buy into this network concept, realize that our strength is in the ability to assimilate into the respective cultures as cohesively as possible.

Your ability to be well liked and respected moves you quickly into accepted-player status, as do your applicable skills. This is reminiscent of the herding concept, discussed in Chapter 1. Those who are charged with granting opportunities for advancement are also looking to promote those who seem to be like themselves. Your flexibility in adopting a balanced attitude and character thus becomes invaluable to your future success. Should you go against this insight and elect to remain rigid in your attitude, you could expect far fewer opportunities to improve your station in life. You will not become a card-carrying member of the networks that control whether or not you may be given a fair shot at future opportunities. Maintaining a rigid attitude is definitely not a good way to leave others feeling.

How many times have you seen the not-so-strange phenomenon of people with weak abilities gaining fortune and prosperity because they are continually being promoted? I believe it is good to be well liked and respected. However, I also believe this becomes far more powerful when you are able to back up that likeability and respect with education, good common sense and a strong work ethic. Both character and content are important tools for building your balanced attitude and creating opportunity. Make no mistake, without good character and a high like-ability factor, you may never earn the opportunity to show what you know!

This notion stands up whether we are speaking about weekend basketball with the boys or weekday power sessions in the boardroom. How you leave others feeling and the perception others have of your character, determine whether or not people include you in their activities. At the end of the day, your ultimate fate will be judged by how you leave others feeling!

Whenever you practice these seven key ways to leave others feeling good, you gain the opportunity to leave people feeling energized. Your positive outlook on life becomes infectious. Other key benefits of using these principles are that others trust and count on you. The final benefit is that your communication skills will be heightened. As I have stated a number of times throughout this book, you gain the best position in life when you use the power of others to help you along. That being said, why not strive for the most balanced attitude to help this process work smoothly? You have everything to gain by subscribing to these principles and by leaving others feeling good about you.

Key Action Steps
The Best Way to Leave People Feeling

Action Step 1
Place yourself in a position to be coachable

"Whenever the student is ready, the teacher will appear."

- Unknown

Remaining coachable is beneficial whether you are in a personal or professional situation. Whenever you are willing to continuously improve, you will find disseminators of information to help you. It's like the old saying: "Whenever the student is ready, the teacher will appear." I have lived this proverb and the best things I have in life are a manifestation of this truth! As long as the assistance from others remains respectful, you must learn to welcome the process because it will serve to shorten your learning curve in life.

Action Step 2
Leave an impression on others that they matter

In this chapter, I state that people like to know that they matter. I also state that the best way to leave people is to leave them wanting more from you. If you combine these two directives you can create a powerful path to leaving others feeling good. Take this time to stop and ponder the three most powerful relationships in your life. Ask yourself these questions: "Do I leave people wanting more of me? Do I leave the three most important people with the impression of how much they matter in my life?" If you find yourself answering no to these two questions, then it is likely that others in your life are probably not receiving due respect from you.

Take this opportunity to make a positive change in how you leave others feeling. Start with your three most powerful relationships, working through to relationships with acquaintances and strangers. You will be surprised and pleased with how your life changes by practicing these principles.

Action Step 3
Apologize at the appropriate times

The apology is probably the most misused and misunderstood tool in the world of interpersonal communication. There are those who overuse the apology to the degree that it simply becomes hollow. This is primarily because of the overuse of the words "I'm sorry." Overuse of this term indicates that a person doesn't really mean the apology. Moreover, whatever behavior caused the apology continues to persist. People in this category use "I'm sorry" to shake off guilt and negative tension, rather than as a means to pay respect and launch an effort of reform.

The other extreme is those who never have it in them to deliver an apology. This is especially hurtful when their words or actions have caused unnecessary damage. These people oftentimes understand the damage caused, but their self-esteem disallows them the humility to apologize. Whenever you find yourself on the wrong side of best intentions, try these two sincere words, "I'm sorry." When delivered with sincerity, an apology becomes something more than damage control. It also makes us feel better about our own human reality. This, not so coincidentally, is a reflection of the truth. We are all full of flaws and the lessons we seek to best correct those flaws lie squarely in the mistakes we make. Regardless of the final outcome, a sincere apology will always leave the other person feeling better.

Action Step 4
Learn to listen well

Are you a good listener? Where do you focus your attention when you are listening to others? As mentioned earlier, eye contact is a good way to prove to the person who is speaking that you are listening. Follow this by occasionally checking for understanding and by paraphrasing parts of the speaker's message.

Become a good listener by demonstrating your ability to remain patient and respectful to those who have the floor during conversation. This patience conveys to the speaker that you value them and leaves a good impression.

Action Step 5
Maintain a responsible and balanced attitude

A balanced attitude makes it far easier to create an approachable persona. You must endeavor to remove the quirks from your personality. In narrow circumstances, possessing a quirky personality may come in handy. However, across broader circumstances, it will leave you sidelined and removed from positive opportunities. You will likely turn off more people than you turn on by owning a quirky personality.

In order to maintain a balanced attitude, you must improve your listening skills, etiquette, interpersonal skills and proactive involvement in all your relationships. Your motto should be to leave every situation better than you found it. Close observance of the initial six key ways to leave others feeling is crucial to your success in maintaining a responsible and balanced attitude, which is the seventh key.

Summary Points
The Best Way to Leave People Feeling

1. Learning from others honors the universal law of giving and receiving

2. Uplift others; share your positive energy; leave them wanting more

3. When you respect others, you leave them knowing that they matter

4. Remembering someone's name leaves them feeling good

5. Nobody is above making mistakes; learn to apologize at the right times

6. Excellent communication starts by becoming a good listener

7. Maintaining a flexible and balanced attitude increases your connections

Affirmations
Moments for Reflection

1. I attract positive and intelligent people to assist my personal development

2. I demonstrate how much others matter by valuing them and by sharing my positive energy

3. I vow to learn the names of people I meet

4. My self-esteem is advanced and allows me to easily apologize for my mistakes

5. I maintain a balanced and flexible attitude, which attracts mavens and connectors to me

Chapter 6

The Third Essential Law of Life
The Law of Personal and Professional Development

The Law of Personal and Professional Development represents the central point of your growth on life's success journey. As noted above, it is the third essential law of life. As I explore this law, consider that personal and professional development will be discussed both separately and concurrently, depending on the perspective being conveyed.

At times, I will offer examples that speak of the personal, while in other instances, I will need to highlight professional matters. Consequently, both personal and professional aspirations converge and create a synergy that propels you forward. Since they always impact one another, we will presuppose the flexibility of alternating their usage interchangeably throughout this book.

As we embark on the quest for understanding the value of using the Law of Personal and Professional Development, take a moment to reflect on the first two essential laws of life, the Law of Attitude and the Law of Communication. In the previous chapters, my main objectives were to examine these laws carefully and endeavor to help you internalize them. Living and breathing the Law of Attitude and accepting and adopting the Law of Communication expand your horizons by giving you the necessary awareness for how to leave others feeling good. Helping others in a proper and respectful fashion is impossible without an innate understanding of the laws of attitude and communication. As noted earlier, helping others get what they want is crucial in order for them to help you get what you want. This knowledge is the perfect segue into understanding the Law of Personal and Professional Development.

The Law of Personal and Professional Development is

a major key to realizing your potential and maximizing growth. With introspection, you can understand who you are, what your gifts are and what your life's purpose is. Subsequently, the Law of Personal and Professional Development will help you discover your life's purpose through the manifestation of your desired reality. This law will challenge you to achieve the life you deserve by first helping you to understand and boost your "deserve level."

Raising your deserve level

Whenever I think of the deserve level, I'm reminded of my friend and client Betty Elliott-Kichler and her husband, Joe Kichler. Elliott-Kichler is a National Sales Director for Mary Kay Cosmetics in Toronto, Canada. She lives her life by helping others discover and live the lives they deserve. She does this by showing them how to evaluate and increase their deserve levels so they accept abundance in their lives. Elliott-Kichler leads her team through the development stages of the Mary Kay marketing system. In fact she calls her unit of Mary Kay, "the Believers." I continue to execute professional speaking seminars for her and the Mary Kay organization. A common conversation that she and I engage in while helping her team, the Believers, is about how to raise their deserve levels.

Your deserve level is the key ingredient for allowing yourself to be comfortable receiving a life of abundance. In other words, if your deserve level is low, meaning that you continue to tell yourself that you don't deserve a better life, you will never allow yourself to sustain complete happiness and a high quality of life. What do I mean by a life of abundance and a high quality of life? Simply put, it means to live a standard of life that consistently makes you happy, supported by a continual flow of ever-increasing spirit.

As easy as it sounds, many people find their efforts

thwarted at the beginning and their lives remain devoid of the most important part - the spark! The spark is knowing where you stand with your deserve level. The key to igniting that spark into a flame is for you to clearly define what it will take to obtain sustained fulfillment and happiness. You must work beyond the point of merely sustaining that energy and leap into creating the desire to do so. When you internalize this thought, you raise your deserve level while boosting the power of the Law of Personal Development.

Should you decide not to improve your deserve level, all of your best efforts to improve your quality of life will be stunted because you continue to embrace self-sabotage - to the point that you no longer have the very thing you desire. This becomes a self-fulfilling prophecy, a never-ending cycle. The quickest way to squash the self-sabotaging effect is to raise your deserve level and continually monitor your position on this point. The human barometer that measures your deserve level must always be in good working order. Make sure your deserve level thermostat is set high enough to be rewarding, but just lower than the level that others perceive as arrogant and self-serving. Setting this thermostat is like observing the mantra that says, "If you are going to go to the ocean and remove water, don't take a teaspoon." It's your life, set the bar high and live up to it!

"If you are going to go to the ocean and remove water, don't take a teaspoon."

- Unknown

Be mindful of that awful notion of scarcity. It is the opposite of abundance and where many people reside. Whenever you allow your mindset to run on scarcity mode you limit your potential. As a result, your quality of life decreases. Think of it this way, scarcity douses out abundance. The author of "The Energy of Money", Maria Nemeth, profiles a wonderful theory of scarcity and its inevitable effects on people's lives.

Oftentimes, it is the memories etched into our minds from our childhood that bring on the notion of scarcity. Many parents use a style of discipline which results in continually telling kids what they can't do. This is the opposite of stressing what they can do. People hear things like: "Don't get too big for your britches", "Who do you think you are?", "What makes you think you are good enough to deserve that?" or "You don't deserve your own bike; you will have to share with your brothers and sisters!"

Parents usually mean no harm, but the continual flow of negative reinforcement is oftentimes what people recall. This family conditioning is what people run on. You must change your programming in order to adjust your deserve-level thermostat.

Five tips for improving your personal development efforts

1. Raise your deserve level

2. Adjust your quality-of-life index and deserve-level thermostat

3. Know yourself

4. Remain open to changing yourself

5. Help shape the perception others have of you

Nurturing and improving your thoughts improve your self-esteem

The best way to improve yourself is to adjust your deserve-level thermostat and quality-of-life index. With clear vision, understand who you are, how you think about yourself and the perception others have of you. There are many ways to arrive at this clarity. The most fundamental path is by nurturing and improving your thoughts, which leads to a positive self-image and high self-esteem.

I have never heard of a case where someone has risen to great heights and sustained any measure of prosperity while possessing low self-esteem. It's important to realize the weighted value that a positive self-image and high self-esteem have on you. Additionally, the quality and character of people you surround yourself with will dramatically affect your entire life continuum. Succinctly said, be careful of the company that you keep because your quality of life depends on it. The following tips will help you get on the right track to improving your thoughts and outlook.

"Be careful of the company that you keep because your quality of life depends on it."

- Jesse Ferrell

Six tips to improving your thoughts and outlook

1. Undertake a directed reading program

2. Maintain the company of quality people in your life

3. Practice daily meditation

4. Repeat positive affirmations

5. Practice creative visualization

6. Allow yourself decompression time

Directed reading program

A good directed reading program consists of a steady diet of books and articles that are either in your field of study or related to your passion. If you are fortunate, your passion is your field of study and you get a two-for-one deal in this area. Set a goal for the number of books or articles you plan to read on a monthly basis and stick to the program. You will derive many benefits from this directive.

Maintaining the company of quality people in your life

Maintaining a program of allowing only quality people in your life will help blow negative people out of your world. One negative comment from a so-called friend can do more damage than a number of positive comments from well-wishers. You don't need any help to think negatively - you can manage this feat on your own. You need others to help you do better. If you can't help one another do better, there is no point in maintaining the relationship.

Daily meditation

Daily meditation is cleansing and therapeutic. You may only have time to manage five minutes of daily meditation. If that is the case, good, just do it! We allow our subconscious minds to bring in more guided messages when we slow our worlds down to a crawl. Remain quiet and open to receiving those messages. If you can manage longer periods of meditation, the benefits are even better. The very best forms of meditation are a mixing of Mother Nature and calm surroundings. This form of meditation increases your connection to source energy.

Positive affirmations

We all deal with an abundance of negative thoughts and interactions. These negative events come in the form of negative self-talk and extend through to toxic people who poison our environments. Whenever you stick to a mental diet of reading positive affirmations, you counterbalance negative thoughts and restore the faith that good things are on the horizon. Positive affirmations help brighten the landscape and change your attitude from feeling down, to feeling up and excited about your life.

Creative visualization

Creative visualization exercises will help you see your path clearly and send powerful messages to your subconscious mind. Your subconscious mind is the best place to plant ideas, concepts and plans of action. This is because it will go to work on ensuring that the instructions you give it are carried out. Just like your breathing continues to function while you are asleep and unaware of it, your subconscious mind keeps on working while you rest. It registers and processes all the impressions and instructions you have fed it. This is the reason for intentionally conveying the messages and instructions to the subconscious mind that will help you live the life you desire.

Decompression time

There will be times when you simply need to unplug! As you manage the daily rigors of life, decompression time can be your best friend. Periodically take time to allow yourself to do nothing except exist. The best places I have found to decompress are in health spas. Additional places to find time to connect body, mind and soul are nature's playgrounds where lakes, oceans, trees, mountains and fresh air can revitalize us.

The very fact that you are reading this book tells me you are the type of person who would benefit from decompression time. People who are constantly looking for the best ways to improve their lives can build in decompression time. This time can save you from depression time, which if allowed to go unchecked, can be followed by psychotherapy time.

Boost your brainpower and feed your intelligence

Your personal development efforts must include a program to boost your brainpower. In order to feed this intelligence, vow to load up on the best grade of fuel and other high-octane additives for a strong mind, body and soul. Your goal should be to maintain maximum brainpower. Many times people refrain from expanding their knowledge as a result of ignorance, fear, apathy or good old-fashioned laziness. You can't afford to allow these tired excuses for lack of action to fill your brain; otherwise, they will run the show.

Like it or not, you will become your thoughts. The most advanced thinkers agree that you become what you think about most of the time. Your thoughts will either create action or allow inaction to be your life's story.

You will learn the benefits of continued growth as a result of expanding your thoughts, knowledge and experiences. Be reminded of what I conveyed from the Law of Communication: "You will be the same person you are now ten years from now, except for the people that you meet, the books that you read and how you manage your own life experiences." This compelling message is worth noting again in the study of the Law of Personal and Professional Development.

If you absorb and embrace these three influential elements, they will do more to shape and revamp your thoughts than anything else you can imagine. There is a distinct and clear correlation between this quote and the person you become. It becomes the best model for improving your signature in life.

Your unique signature shapes perception

The people you meet, the books you read and the way you manage your life experiences formulate the indelible ink of your unique signature - the mark of how you do things, which is left behind once you have moved on. In fact, your ultimate goal in exploring the Law of Personal and Professional Development is to bring about a call-to- action in all three of the key areas. This opens the way to positive and continuous development in your life.

We discussed the value of leaving your signature behind by observing the Law of Communication in Chapter 4 and it also merits repeating here in the Law of Personal and Professional Development. By developing and controlling the message that your signature conveys, you shape the perception that others have of you. And it is impossible to overstate the importance of perception. Because other people's perceptions become your reality, your personal and professional development rides on your willingness to change and ability to adapt to new situations. This is necessary in order to maintain others' positive perception of you. Thus you are shaping your own image - rather than accepting someone else's spin on your reality.

In other words, if you maintain good relations, your personal signature will be an attractive one and it will shape people's perceptions of you in a positive way. You will thus be following the golden rule of the Law of Personal and Professional Development: Always leave others feeling good about you!

The Law of Personal and Professional Development is the utility player

The Law of Personal and Professional Development runs through all of the other essential laws of life. You might view this law as the utility ball player in the game of life. The analogy is to the major-league baseball player who is so talented and versatile, that he can play all positions on the field, as well as having specialty positions. For example, while you may be exercising the Law of Attitude in putting your best foot forward to gain employment, you can't help but be supported by the Law of Personal and Professional Development. These two laws are synergistically connected.

Conversely, someone who has disrespected the Law of Personal and Professional Development and failed to grow in this area, will not be honoring the Law of Attitude either. It will be evident to others that a lack of personal and professional development is reflected in the job seeker's attitude. He or she may have the best skills on the market, but if their attitude signals trouble, they may never be given the opportunity to show what they know.

The best reason to strive for growth in the area of personal and professional development is to improve yourself by creating harmony among your mental, physical and spiritual natures. Additionally, this harmony manifests as an easy disposition, which makes you attractive and charismatic. Using charisma to leave others feeling good is fun and rewarding for both you and the recipient. This charisma also allows you to communicate effectively with others. And this effective communication is important in working with and through, others in order to do your best work.

The Law of Personal and Professional Development also shares an integral and interesting connection with the Law of Communication. Among the objectives for increasing successful communication are sustained growth and development. A keen understanding of communication and the power of words builds a solid foundation for your personal development. This synergy, in turn, creates unstoppable achievement. Within this chapter, I will continue to explore the Law of Personal and Professional Development in depth, along with the Law of Communication. I believe their benefits to be integrally related.

Will you choose personal and professional development?

At the risk of sounding redundant, I can't stress enough the importance and relevance of the Law of Personal and Professional Development. This law will truly make or break you! Should you take it lightly or opt to ignore it, you will significantly affect your life in a negative fashion! I can personally attest to this. In 1997, my choice to ignore this law broke me because I chose to focus on climbing the corporate ladder and placed the highest value on my career. I neglected prudent and healthy personal and professional development choices. Basically, my priorities were left unchecked and remained out of sorts. At that time, I wasn't working for a living - I was living to work and the corporate machine loves to entice people like me into the system. My strong desire to succeed and to compete at the highest level, along with a case of "overachiever mentality," made me a natural acquisition for the insatiable corporate machine.

I don't think it was the eighteen-hour workdays and twenty-four-hour, on-call status that caused my slide into oblivion and extreme burnout. Rather, it was the lack of attention to self and the extreme neglect of personal development that propelled the largest slide into nothingness that I could have ever imagined. I simply placed my health and growth as the last priority while failing to realize the resultant damage and downward spiral effect. This oversight ultimately manifested in brain overload and a life of chaos. With things becoming so mixed up, you might say I had an extreme case of the tail wagging the dog!

Put another way, I was in what I call "brain freeze" - scrambled connections and reduced functioning due to being deprived of the proper rest and nourishment. You will encounter times when you believe you should clearly know the answer to a simple question and your brain freezes up and disallows an intelligent response: This is brain freeze.

With brain freeze, your brain's axons and dendrites are not allowed to fire electrical thought strikes across to one another, which is the way thoughts are connected. This of course feels like your brain is short-circuiting. The final symptom of this is burnout. This stems from physical, mental and spiritual depletion. When you allow all systems to run on information overload for too long, in an overly demanding environment, you cannot escape the effects of burnout and brain freeze. And it is all too clear how circumstances like this would leave you feeling!

Maintaining the proper health and attitude begins with ordering your priorities in a prudent manner. That is, you improve yourself and your ability to assist others around you when you place your physical, mental and spiritual health in the first position of priorities. This is accomplished by developing a continual state of mental, physical and spiritual balancing, which is critical for maintaining a rewarding life. There is a definite connection between personal and professional development. My story of burnout proves this powerful synergistic relationship. Your determination to preserve balance is the best way to leave yourself feeling good. Ultimately you will lay the foundation for leaving others feeling good too.

Two-for-ones and three-for-ones lead to good professional development

In addition to the need to maintain personal balance, there are other key factors that promote your professional development. Your efforts in this regard are best helped by learning and maintaining good time-management and organizational skills. The ability to execute and access information in a timely fashion will set you apart from the rest. Good time-management skills also create opportunities for getting more done during your work hours. I love to get a "two-for-one" or even a "three-for-one" on my task-management mission.

What is a two-for-one or a three-for-one? This is when

a single action serves two or three other functions. For instance, whenever I must drive to an appointment, I always listen to a pertinent audio book to and from my appointment. This offers the safety of getting to my destination without becoming involved in "road rage" as a result of traffic delays. I also move my reading program forward by listening to audio books while I drive. This is a classic example of a three-for-one while maximizing my time to the fullest degree. Your aim should always lean toward developing successful actions.

Time-management and organizational skills are very closely related. Learning how to prioritize your commitments helps you stay centered and focused on always doing the most important tasks first. In an effort to create a task-management strategy, some people will make themselves a "to-do" list. And in some cases people have a number of to-do lists with some of the tasks scratched off on each one. Although a fair attempt at organization, this becomes quite confusing and most of the time you can't find the list you are looking for.

To end this confusion, I created a master organizational system called DAAL (Daily Accelerated Action List), which manages a world of shifting priorities for busy executives. You are directed to maintain this single list. This system is based in a Microsoft Excel program. It encompasses priorities, due dates, an action-items category, an aging date, date-done functions and a task history. All of these are archived at the click of a button. The ability to sort the list by the categories noted above is what drives the acceleration of the DAAL. Most to-do lists that others make are stagnant and unable to be rearranged in a split second. Instead the DAAL gives you options such as dividing up five different lists, with a chronological focus. Please review examples of the DAAL and DAAL benefits on the following pages.

DAAL BENEFITS

Key Points	KEY DAAL BENEFITS
1	Master Organizational System - designed for task management - projects that have minor to major impact
2	Shifting Priorities - Rank and priority system allowing you to manage a world of shifting priorities
3	Creative Thinking - Dedicated use of the DAAL adds a major assist in clearing your mind of remembering small to large tasks
4	Set The Table - The DAAL is constantly executing and re-setting the table (priority sense) indicating best time management
5	Turn Off & On The Lights - DAAL allows you to call it a day and know you have not left something time sensitive on the table
6	Turn On The Lights - Get Ready, DAAL leaves your table already pre-set for the next days activity without re-organizing
7	Team Player - DAAL is a team player working well with other peripherals, I.e, hand held PDA's, laptops, computers, etc.
8	Time Saver - The find command and history component helps saving time when needing to verify specific information
9	Discipline Discretion Tool - You can clearly see at a glance what tasks need to be done in relation to others, just by it's design
10	Triple Your Time - DAAL allows you to cluster, related items and resolve to completion by networking like tasks
11	Deadline Targets Hit - DAAL forces you to hit your deadlines if you respect the DAAL in full
12	Aging Report - DAAL offers an aging report that lets you sort by the date the item hit your DAAL and filter out unimportant tasks
13	Navigational Ease - DAAL offers time saving functions for quick info sorts and next due requests
14	Accelerated by the ranking, aging function, due date features, acts as more than a list
15	Action - Highest priority tasks are always being shuffled into action and since of accomplishment can be reviewed at a glance
16	What gets measured gets done!

ACTION TASKS

RANK	DATE	GROUP	CONTACT	ASSIST	ACTION TASKS DESCRIPTION	DUE	DONE
2	04/17/06		Pam	Pam	Stewart Hall make the connection and set up the June trip - with travel plans and everything	05/13/06	
1	03/02/06		Victoria	Tony	Get Victoria - publicity photo, bio and what my business does	05/14/06	
2	04/29/06		Jason	Allen	update the book counts from pre-order book	05/14/06	
2	05/12/06	HYLTF	Don	Allen	Dr. Elliott Jaques Requisite Organization - Don Schminke (Jerry Harvey the Aboline Paradox, the gun smoke phenomina)	05/14/06	
1	12/27/05	JessTalk	Jesse	Jesse	Add Financial section to my JessTalk Lifestyle Portfolio and add 1st start of	05/15/06	
1	04/05/06				Mike - email him with options for coaching slot, find his business card given to me in Dominican Republic	05/15/06	
1	04/14/06		Ann		Ann Lee wants me to check cut sagaworldwide.com (Don Schmenke) I need to review tech and speakers on ipod	05/15/06	
1	04/23/06		Rob		Business Expo - give away and follow up piece - build the booth How You Leave Them Feeling/JessTalk Rob	05/15/06	
1	05/01/06				Update William Campbell business address on mailing list	05/15/06	
1	05/08/06				Darryl Odom - send frame work for JessTalk book campaign soon	05/15/06	
1	05/09/06				Tony Robins find West coast dates and book for within the next 90 days - George Foreman	05/15/06	
1	05/09/06	Martin	Ann Lee		Ann and Jess to do presentation run through bring high lighter to show Ann and Jess mark - need to fine tune power point	05/15/06	
1	05/09/06	Martin	Ann Lee		Video tape of Curt and Jesse handing off the training - videoagrapher talk about handoff sessions	05/15/06	
2	11/11/05				Book - Barnes check for book campaign with Community Relations Manager	05/15/06	
2	01/25/06	HYLTF	Jack		WH Smith books stores - representative in each book store for book signing flying across the (partners, airline, hotel, etc.) country	05/15/06	
2	02/24/06	HYLTF	Jesse		How You Leave Them Feeling business cards - from the author - simple message on the back and how to order	05/15/06	
2	04/25/06				The Purple Cow and Selling the invisible books recommended by Chamber Executive - must buy	05/15/06	
2	05/08/06	HYLTF			Letters from return mail - update and clean up database for 3rd tier drop	05/15/06	
2	05/09/06				Business Expo - give away and follow up piece - Robert Heidt. Jr. 641-5822	05/15/06	
3	01/24/06			Jesse	Car Milage - do some catch up work	05/15/06	
1	04/27/06				Package prep and write intro letter to Roe (Bybee contact) prepare package to be delivered ASAP	05/16/06	
5	10/30/05				Sky-Office 5-Must Do's 1) coaching shuffle 2) JessTalk Lifestyle Portfolio roll	05/17/06	
2	10/24/05	HYLTF	Jesse	Jesse	Book research, read articles on best way to promote a new book, find out	05/20/06	

TASKS HISTORY

RANK	DATE	GROUP	CONTACT	ASSIST	ACTION TASKS DESCRIPTION	DUE	DONE
1	02/21/06	HYLTF	Lori	Jason	Send chapter 9 to lori Burley	02/21/06	02/22/06
1	02/22/06	Al & Nate			Seattle based concept - the Great Northwest Bar and Grill (working title) Northwest microbrews USP	02/22/06	02/22/06
1	02/22/06	Al & Nate			Nate & Allen - has investors for the bar and grill (has expertise and need some othe experts)	02/22/06	02/22/06
1	02/01/06	Tahoe	Patty	Debra	Create spread sheet for gifts, amenities, events/activitites rooms etc. and send to Patty	02/23/06	02/24/06
1	02/22/06	Al & Nate			email deserve level, absolute codes and book recommendations	02/23/06	02/23/06
1	02/24/06	HYLTF			Rob Ciccone bullet point list of Fire Side Chat	02/24/06	02/24/06
1	10/14/05	HYLTF	Rob	Mary	Book -prepare Data base for Robert Ciccone - email, dreamhost, old excel file	02/26/06	03/01/06
1	02/07/06	Tahoe			Print out Boarding Passes for Kim in Tahoe and yourself in Houston	02/26/06	03/01/06
1	03/02/06	Chamber	Victoria		booth registration for June 7, 2006 (also look at how I can submit an article)	03/10/06	03/02/06
1	03/02/06	Chamber	Victoria		lvchamber.com\expo	03/10/06	03/02/06
1	03/02/06	Chamber	Victoria		Young Professionals Group - Last Friday of the month 10 times (Leadership Las Vegas)	03/10/06	03/15/06
1	03/13/06	Elliott			Elliott Ferrell pitstop - Magic of Believing - think and grow rich -drive by/whole foods - best buy	03/15/06	03/22/06
1	03/13/06	Elliott			Drew Elliott send JessTalk video package for personal use to corp Orangeville	03/15/06	03/22/06
1	03/02/06	Chamber	Victoria		Chamber events - calendar of events, call Victoria and ask which ones I should go to	03/25/06	03/20/06
1	03/12/06	Elliott			Ocean Side Chat at the Villa (Teddy to cater) offer it at VIP Keynote - sign ups so we know	04/01/06	04/01/06
1	03/13/06	Elliott			Bring down 12 manuscripts signed for Derek's team	04/01/06	04/01/06
1	03/02/06	Chamber	Victoria		Ladies that come with convention goers would enjoy a lunch with the coach type of deal/Victorias idea	05/25/06	05/01/06
2	01/29/06	Casino	Jim		He sent email re: upcoming trip, see casino marketing archive - book golf and get back to Jim with final	03/15/06	03/15/06
2	01/25/06	HYLTF	Jesse		Tahoe fireside chat - use the JessTalk virtual office to have others sign in (check w/dave about limit) live broadcast	03/18/06	03/20/06

Anytime a task hits my plate, it receives an immediate priority ranking of one to five. One is the highest priority and typically date-sensitive, while five is the least priority and the least date-sensitive. After loading in the newest tasks and assigning their priority, with the click of a button, the task is re-sorted in with all prior tasks related to its level of priority. I focus on using my time to expedite task management for the level-one and level-two priorities, while all task levels of three to five get done whenever time permits and according to their due dates. This system buys me more time for creative thinking than anything else I can imagine.

I load small to important tasks into the DAAL and let the system guide me as to what tasks should be done and in what order. We all enjoy crossing tasks off our lists: however, the DAAL affords me the luxury of crossing off the highest priority tasks off the list first. One click of the history task function and the completed tasks shift over to the history archives, thus creating a permanent record of task resolution and lessening my to do-list all at once. It is a great feeling to see the action task list shrink in a world of shifting priorities. The DAAL system itself yields three-for-one's in its design.

A steady DAAL diet of task management will raise the bar on your professionalism. If you aren't using a system like DAAL, you are making your professional life much tougher than it needs to be. DAAL always leaves me confident that I'm proactively managing my professional world and this leaves me feeling good!

As noted earlier in this chapter, personal development and professional development are closely tied to one another. Oftentimes, the principles you practice in your personal life leak over and blend into the value system you construct in your professional life and vice versa. For this very reason I created a tool to manage the overlapping synergies. This tool is called the JessTalk Lifestyle Portfolio. The aim of this tool is to manage your strategic life plan, while housing everything from your long-term, ten-year perspective down through your 90-day action plan. The sections are customized to each individual so you can maintain order in your JessTalk Lifestyle Portfolio. See the examples to follow.

In order to obtain maximum clarity and focus, I have assembled and created a few systems that will manage your entire world of obligations, both personal and professional. The systems created by JessTalk Speaking Services are intended to work efficiently with Microsoft products. I have bundled these systems into an office suite that I refer to as SIS (Simply Integrated Systems). SIS consists of the following office suite tools:

SIS - Simply Integrated Systems

1. Microsoft Outlook: manage email, contacts and calendar appointments

2. DAAL: daily accelerated action list, my task management system

3. JessTalk Lifestyle Portfolio: life road map - the plan

4. Pocket PC - PDA: backs up all systems above and is a convenient pocket size

Please see a typical layout of the different sectors housed in a JessTalk Lifestyle Portfolio to follow.

JessTalk Lifestyle Portfolio

1. 90 day Plan (daily goals and objectives to be measured in 90 days)

2. 1 Year Outlook (looking closely at where you see your life in one year)

3. 5 Year Perspective (long-term vision of your life five years from now)

DAILY CHECK-IN

Priority	Master Communications Network	Period
1	Quantum Strength Pilars - review % power, revise and stay connected with pillar strength and grow	Daily
1	Ferrell Financial Group - review and update as needed	Daily
1	President's Report - Lifestyle Portfolio	Monthly
1	Book - Write the book during prime time hours - 2 hours daily	Daily
1	Articles - Continue to produce monthly articles (generate idea listing)	Weekly
1	Voice Mail - Daily Maintenance - cell - phonekate - home phone	Daily
1	Call at least one key customer daily	Daily
2	Write at least one letter to known customers per day (Mon - Fri) only	Daily

	JessTalk Operations - Day In A Life Schedule	
Sunday	Meditation, Fun & Rest (2 hours daily reading)	1
Monday	Marketing Package mail outs - Focus - Normal Daily Operations (1 hour daily reading)	2
Tuesday	Normal Daily Operations - Full Push Focus - 8 hours (1 hour daily reading)	3
Wednesday	Decompression Day (1 hour daily reading)	4
Thursday	Normal Daily Operations - Full Push Focus - 8 hours (1 hour daily reading)	5
Friday	Bonus Flex day - 6 hours (1 hour daily reading)	6
Saturday	Technical Office Equipment Training 2 hours - Anything Goes Reading Program - 2 hours	7

	Travel With Section
1	Laptop
2	Cell Phone/Beeper
3	PDA
4	Personal Transfer Files
5	Special Assignment Items
6	JessTalk Promotional Materials

90 DAY PLAN

Point	Category		
			Chief Aim in Life - Critical Results Area
			Major definite purpose: My purpose is to help as many people as I possibly can through advanced vehicles of communication
			I will focus my energy on living upto the person I imagine and seeking expression of this through meditation, prayer & belief
	3 Quarterly Prime Objectives		
			1) Leveraging Assets (People, Money, Time, Results from Life Experiences, Educational Growth Moments)
			2) Simplifying Systems, Processes & Communications
			3) Best Time Management Models - Best Practices Rolled In
1	**Health & Wealth Plan**		Must maintain bio-balance through proper workouts, eating plan, reading and discriminating people exposure plan
	Bio-Environmentally		Financial Freedom must be obtained through the pillar power and relationship marketing campaigns
	Balanced Lifestyle		1) I work out 5 - 6 days per week - basketball, tennis, roller blades, running/walking
			2) I take a decompression day once per month - fluff & buff at J.W. Marriott
			3) I remain faithful to my personal tax commitment (20 % of all earning must be transferred into the Life Plan Account at the point of acquisition)
		1st Qtr. 94.44%	4) My revenue goals, has exceeded my goal of 20% increases on a quarterly basis
		2nd Qtr. 83.33%	5) I continue to review and manage Quantum Strength Pillars and search for more passive income streams
		3rd Qtr. 88.89%	6) I micromanage expenses in effort to retain as much cash as possible toward the purchase of new company car
		4th Qtr. 100.00%	7) I have found the avenues leading to $10,000 in monthly discretionary income
			8) I attract personal and professional development clients (maximum of 6 new clients per 90 day cycle)
			9) I have increased Standard Radio from 3 years to 4 years – Critical Wealth Radio from 8 years to 10 years
			10) I expedite my Help A Stranger Program - select one unknown person who needs help and deliver just the right help needed (once per month)
			11) I donate $100 U.S. Aid - Donation of $100 per trip to a well deserving Dominican family
			12) I laugh more this period, find avenues of laughter through friends, movies, comedy cd's, self laughter, (I mean laugh out loud more) A good belly laugh!
			13) I have a personal fitness trainer. (1 day per week work out with trainer - 2 additional strength training days) goal improve body symmetry
			14) I no longer conduct sport eating events, anytime I think of eating for sport, the food must be replaced by 16 0unces of water
			15) I maintain no more than a 17.4% body fat (22.7% is gone forever)
			16) I keep my waistline at 34 inches or less
			17) I take a Personal Enrichment Advance day - One full day of concentrated positive thinking leading to positive doing day (quiet day)
			18) I take one day per month to concentrate my full day on being thankful, respectful and reflect upon the many gifts I have received
2	**Maximum Exposure Plan**		Quantum Leap exposure of JessTalk by executing tasks below - #1 mission is to create a word of mouth epidemic marketing style
	Elevator Speech		'How You Leave Them Feeling' becomes the ultimate model of bust-out exposure & making synergistic contact with various archetypes & charismatic leaders
			1) I am a published author as of 2nd quarter of 2006
			2) I write monthly JessTalk articles for Elliott/Sun Village and JessTalk 'How You Leave Them Feeling' database - load on website
		1st Qtr. 90.91%	3) I conduct book tours/speaking engagements - pre-launch * launch & post launch of 'How You Leave Them Feeling'
		2nd Qtr. 90.00%	4) I do internet radio, traditional radio (John Derringer Toronto Canada) television and print interviews for 'How You Leave Them Feeling' campaign
		3rd Qtr. 80.00%	5) I tour all the major cities where I have key contacts to fill a room - Vegas, Toronto, Vancouver, Houston, Los Angeles, New York, Portland, Orlando
		4th Qtr. 90.00%	6) I continue to edit the How You Leave Them Feeling book during prime time hours
			7) I contact other successful speakers and ask them how they made the leap from looking for places to speak to having more requests than they can handle
			8) I stay in touch with Louis Gossett Jr. in order to help him on his Farm and Eracism campaigns
			9) I connect Louis Gossett Jr. with the Elliott's and the Navy Island investment project - love of Louis (retirement plan)
			10) I have joined NSA in order to gain accreditation and more speaking engagements
			11) I make further efforts to connect with the best leadership in my international global village

1ST QUARTER - 90 DAY PLAN REPORT CARD

Point	Plan Category	MAX	% earned	Grade	Weight	Value	Supportive Explanation
1	Health & Wealth	4%	4%	94	4	376	Very good focus on workout program, getting proper rest and revenue projections
2	Maximum Exposure Plan	4%	4%	90	4	360	Hosted several international village events, pushed relationship marketing
3	Education and Knowledge Plan	4%	4%	72	4	288	Failed to take full action in this category regarding Spanish commitment and memory program
4	Coaching Initiatives	3%	3%	100	3	300	Continuing to push the bar on the coaching aspects and how to move clients toward goal attainment
5	Discovery	3%	3%	100	3	300	I discovered a number of ways to wow my clients and remainec open for new speaking concepts
6	CEO Profile	2%	2%	94	2	188	The CEO category has achieved h gh marks based on extreme focus on all the major areas
7	Organizational Development	2%	0%	100	2	200	I continue using current systems of measure, both DAAL and Lifestyle Portfolio to guide my effort
8	Personal Enrichment	1%	1%	100	1	100	I practice this area more than ever
9	Lifestyle Transition	1%	0%	100	1	100	My life is continuing to evolve
10	Asking For Help	1%	0%	100	1	100	I have learned to accept help from my global village

90-Day Scoring Index   25% | 21% | 95 | 3 | 231

Grade = Measure of raw achievement, based on performance of individual plan objectives

Weight = Measure of importance of category 5 = highest weight, 1 = lowest weight

Value = Scoring index, combination of grade & weight, the higher the value, the greater the impact

500% = 500% Club - 5 Year goal to increase growth and personal deve opment/effectiveness by 500%

Grade Average High Value Categories =	85
Grade Average For All Categories =	95
Highest % obtainable per quarter =	25%
90 Day Plan % growth achieved =	21%

500% rule - 80% = 1/2 credit & 90% = full credit

1 YEAR OUTLOOK

Order	Rank	Value	Plan Objectives	Why These Goals Are Important	What Kind of person must I become to reach goals
1	1	1	I'm loyal to my God	To be more connected to the source	Spiritual, believer, reader, open to new experiences
2	1	1	I remain Bio balanced (Bio environmentally balanced)	Maintain the best physical and mental health -constant readiness	maintain the best desire to learn & grow, accept new ways of doing things
3	1	1	I change others lives by sharing my best energy	Ability to help more people in a time efficient fashion	Must continue to be patient with others
4	2	2	I produce a minimum of 12 JessTalk videos per year	To grow as a speaker while creating maximum exposure	must attract the decision makers to my charisma and products
5	1	1	I consistently effect others lives positively	Help improve our environment one person at a time	Must become powerful educator and strong communicator
6	1	1	I keep my body, mind and soul crystal clearly focused	Sharp focus is the set up for all good things to follow (cornerstone	Deliberate with clear intentions
7	1	1	I maintain a healthy body mind and spirit	To create a biobalanced state of being	One who seeks continual improvement
8	2	2	I continue to help restore ideal health for my clients	Increase the quality of their health plan	Patient and helpful
9	2	2	I help clients enjoy their new found health	Dramatically improve their outlook and restore full quality of life	Very patient and strategic sharing information
10	1	1	I consistently Lead Leaders	To assure my talents and abilities are appreciated and stimulated	Strong, consistent, clear and concise communicator
11	3	3	I have developed 5th absolute code - psychic energy	This level represents the highest level of energy transmission	I continue to surround myself with influences who own this power
12	2	2	I have learned to write creatively, effectively & passionately	To reach other audiences who may be helped by my message	Continue the practice of writing and securing help to improve
13	1	1	My relationship marketing skills are creating great synergy	To surround myself with the best people	I must continue to grow my energies to attract the best people
14	1	1	I create a business that helps to change others lives	Helping and changing people is therapeutic and also helps me	Willing to give without looking for instant payback
15	2	2	I have a dedicated mentor who helps re-shape my world	Mentors save you years of trial and error	Open for the occurrence and welcoming when they arrive
16	2	2	I have published in the United States and abroad	Exposure helps create a dynamic and charismatic presence	Have a mindset that can handle the demand of others
17	1	1	My energies are resonating at high energy levels	To move through time and space attracting just the right people	Must be attractive & charismatic to pull like minded people to me
18	2	2	I have rewarded my village 10 fold	To lock in my full appreciation for their commitment to JessTalk	Never forgetting their commitment to JessTalk
19	2	2	I discover a new good friend by year end	Good friends are hard to come by	I must become a good friend to someone else first
20	1	1	I stay in top shape, muscular and excellent posture	To keep my energies resonating at high levels	dedicated and focused on eating plan and type of exercise
	1.5	1.45	Totals		

Rank Legend

1	Highest Importance
2	High Importance
3	Important
4	Modestly Important
5	Helpful

Value Legend

1	Highest Value & Impact
2	High Value and Impact
3	Important Value & Impact
4	Modestly Valuable
5	Significant

5 YEAR PERSPECTIVE

Order	Rank	Value	Plan Objectives	Why These Goals Are Important	What Kind of person must I become to reach goals
1	1	2	I discover new talent and help them get it	To help others move up as I have been helped by a few	clear vision and presence of mind
2	3	2	I have dramatically improve societies	To leave a legacy	Must become a world traveler and world class speaker
3	1	1	I consistently affect others lives positively	Help improve our environment one person at a time	Must become powerful educator
4	1	2	I have effectively helped my brothers and sisters	To stimulate positive growth in the family	caring family member who makes time for others
5	2	2	I have found a way to make fathers life complete	Respect the gift of life	Must carve out times to meet with father (lunch once/month)
6	2	2	I have found a way to make mother happy	Respect the gift of life	Must carve out times to meet with father (lunch once/month)
7	1	1	I have become precision focused on all important matters	To attract the brightest minds to me	Very aggressive reader, bio balance d, infectious personality
8	1	2	I'm well known for being a great strategist	To help my clients solve complex issues and chart good paths	Well read, enormous experience
9	1	2	I have discovered the best gifts of life	It is important to learn this message and share it	One who can let go and enjoy, willing to try new things, explore
10	1	1	I have an occupation which allows me to speak all 5 languages	Communicate at a higher level reaching international audiences	Must be easy to be around
	1.40	1.70	Totals		

Rank Legend

1	Highest Importance
2	High Importance
3	Important
4	Modestly Important
5	Helpful

Value Legend

1	Highest Value & Impact
2	High Value and Impact
3	Important Value & Impact
4	Modestly Valuable
5	Significant

10 YEAR VISION

Order	Rank	Value	Plan Objectives	Why These Goals Are Important	What Kind of person must I become to reach goals
1	2	2	Move others with my writing	To become a more effective communicator	I must continue to just write
2	2	2	live in multiple countries	Become more worldly	I remain open to change
3	1	2	Own multiple businesses that change others life	Growing enriching feelings and sharing the experiences	I must work instinctively and create new ways of doing things
4	1	1	Payback all my mentors 100 fold	Pay it forward program	Never forget the power of my global village
5	1	1	Payback my clients 100 fold	Pay it forward program	Never forget the power of my global village
6	2	2	Private Jet to spoil my associates and close partners	this allows me to have fun by sharing exciting gifts with others	I must fully understand the reason for the gift is to share it
7	1	1	Set many new paradigms in creative thinking	To help bring about positive change	I must remain clear and focused, surrounded by other positive lights
8	2	2	Publish in 100 other countries	This broadens the scope of helping hand reaching across waters	Affluent
9	1	2	Re-define Leadership	There is no reason we have to keep the same archetypes	I must learn from the masters while creating a new model
10	1	1	I resonate at high energy levels	This energy is therapeutic to all others, even with noconversation	This supports my help as many people as I can theory
	1.4	1.6	Totals		

Rank Legend	
1	Highest Importance
2	High Importance
3	Important
4	Modestly Important
5	Helpful

Value Legend	
1	Highest Value & Impact
2	High Value and Impact
3	Important Value & Impact
4	Modestly Valuable
5	Significant

AFFIRMATIONS

Count	Powerful Affirmations
1	My life change is God's choice, willingly!
2	I have improved my organizational skills exponentially!
3	My total health is dramatically improved as a direct result of this life change
4	I'm not late in making this change, it has come at just the right time!
5	DAAL is totally developed and being sold throughout the U.S. and other countries under JessTalk
6	I'm the number one speaker in the world
7	I follow the path determined by God
8	I have the power of the Matrix behind me
9	My time management techniques are off the charts successful and highly sought after
10	Leaders of major companies and countries are waiting in line for my time & JessTalk products

Count	Motivation For Maintaining Strong Professional Development Plan
1	Stop wasting time
2	Increase life balance (bio-environmentally balanced)
3	Learn time management techniques to maximize my time and become more efficient
4	Gain maximum clarity
5	Help build stronger relationships

4. 10 Year Vision (longer-term vision of your life ten years from now)

5. Inspiration & Mantras (positive and creative words to feed the brain)

6. Motives List & Affirmations (tools to affirm your chosen lifestyle)

7. Library (important reading to help you along your journey)

8. Mastermind List (a special group of advisors and trusted mentors)

9. Vision Quest 500 (a program measuring your goal for 500% improvement)

The JessTalk Lifestyle Portfolio system brings clarity

For those looking for ongoing guidance, the JessTalk Lifestyle Portfolio is an invaluable asset. With it, you can:

- Gain better clarity and focus on what you want in life
- Enhance fulfillment and meaning in your life
- Secure your future by a change in life direction
- Develop a match between your livelihood and direction in life
- Establish a priority system so that you have time to enjoy the pleasures of life
- Learn to balance stress and overwhelming personal and professional situations
- Improve your overall skills in order to recapture time for yourself
- Take the leap from crisis management to proactive planning
- Learn new organizational skills, which ultimately simplify your life

- Learn creative and fun ways to enjoy enhanced communication
- Change negative, problematic thinking to thinking that allows you to see problems as opportunities

Benefits of using the JessTalk Lifestyle Portfolio

When you use the JessTalk Lifestyle Portfolio, the benefits to you include:

- The opportunity to build your own personal mission statement
- Developing lifestyle plans to manage your personal and professional life
- Expanding your network of awesome resources through a personal growth plan
- Building a profile that challenges you to improve your own life expectations
- Tailoring a program that is custom-designed to fit your personal needs
- Progress reports so you can monitor goal attainment

The scores of JessTalk clients who use the systems above report great relief in their organizational, time-management and life-development planning. You can still derive wonderful benefits from modeling these systems without being in an official coaching program. I encourage you to use this information to make prudent changes in the planning of your development process.

Strategic planning is so important to your overall success that I have included an article I wrote, which is devoted to a style of planning called backwards planning. Do you recall that old adage, "If you fail to plan, plan to fail?" It is a fact that prudent and concise planning is the most important ingredient to include on any success journey. To work your plan from a long-term vision, moving backwards to present time, paints the clearest picture of how you should progress. Please take special note of the article I wrote on the following pages

"If you fail to plan, plan to fail."

- Unknown

regarding the backwards planning concept.

Backwards Planning

"We must use time as a tool, not as a crutch."
- JFK

Time, as measured in seconds, hours, days or even years is the same for everyone. However, how time is perceived is much different. Is it friend or foe? Time, a faithful companion of consistency, can serve as a loyal ally or clever adversary. Time can both sneak up and blind-side you, or act as a guide that navigates you from one task to another. Time is everyone's most valuable resource. How it's used and managed can often determine success or failure.

"What may be done at any time, will be done at no time."

- Unknown

Effective backwards planning is a time management technique that provides the structure and organization needed to successfully complete tasks. A simple concept, often overlooked by most, is to start at the end, determine dates, times and critical concerns and create an action task list that uses shifting priorities as the highlighting feature. This is a system that ensures that the highest-level tasks are done first.

A shifting priorities system is based on two key factors: time sensitivity and a project-dependent completion order. The realization of certain sub-tasks needing to be completed in order to accomplish the job is normally the part of project management that stumps most folks. Strictly adhering to a shifting-priorities action list recovers many hours of simply deciding what to do next, when to do it and how long you should spend executing the various sub-tasks. Ultimately, time is the coach that maintains your focus and discipline. It prepares you for a target goal. Time constraints should not be intimidating show-stoppers. Deadlines are no more than end-lines in a successful and well-orchestrated backwards plan.

The time needed to complete a task is minimized when backwards thinking is employed. In other words, going from point Z to point A is more efficient than going from A to Z. By backtracking from task completion, you will understand what key steps are necessary to complete your final objective. The line is much straighter when you plan from Z to A. When the absence of backwards planning is evident, the culprit most often tends to be shortsighted missteps when moving to point C or impulsive excursions to D or F. These notions can be avoided by effectively using backwards planning. A backwards-planning map will keep you streamlined and focused against time and mission lapses.

Backwards planning should also be used for longer-term goals or projects. Where do you want to be financially or career-wise five years from now? How do you get there? What is your current 90-day plan? Backwards planning keeps you on track. Sub-tasks and checklists demand self-assessment. You should periodically ask yourself, if I'm not where I should be at a predetermined checkpoint, what can I do to get there? Effective time management motivates goal attainment. Planning-ignorance fosters complacency, which is a place where time and achievement move at different speeds.

Key Action Steps
The Law of Personal and Professional Development

Action Step 1
Nurture and improve your mental attitude

The best way to be clear about the path you should take in life is to harness your mental attitude. It is also important to take inventory of your friendships and other interpersonal connections. Check in on the types of relationships you have developed thus far. If there are any draining or toxic relationships in either your personal or your professional life, now is the time to get rid of them! Yes, in order to nourish the best mental attitude, you must blow out tired, poisonous relationships! They take a heavy toll on your self-esteem and well-being. Remember to prepare yourself ahead of the game before omitting those relationships that may be tied to your ability to earn a living. Create a comprehensive transition plan to map out the road that leads to other income.

When it comes to cutting out relationships in your life, the work gets easier if the contact is not helping you do better - that is, if the relationship is in some way hampering you. You will not require anyone's help in making mistakes and doing poorly; we can do poorly all by ourselves! You should correct or replace the toxic relationships, no matter their tenure, with new mutually beneficial relationships. The length of time you have been friends with someone is not always the best way to measure the strength of the relationship. The quality of the relationship alone should be the measuring stick. Every correction or respectful elimination of a relationship that is not consistent with your standards is a big step toward nurturing and improving your mental attitude. This will leave you feeling great!

Action Step 2
Evaluate self - raise your deserve level

Take a close assessment of your strengths and weaknesses. Evaluate your gifts and determine the connection between your gifts and your life's purpose. As a result of the work you complete in Action Step 1 above, measure your mental attitude and weigh in on your deserve level. As you proceed on your development journey, be sure to remain open to change. Having an open mind with respect to change will expedite your learning and development curve on this journey.
Never allow your outlook in life to be negatively influenced by others. Carefully choose the books that you read and invest your valuable time in those readings that move you forward. Become passionate about your

life plan and take the time to enhance it. Most people spend more time planning a one-week vacation than they spend planning their lives.

Schedule time for daily meditation, positive affirmations and creative visualization. Always have at least one day during the week where you have scheduled down time; this means you do absolutely nothing: no television, internet or anything else that begs for your brain's attention. Your outlook will remain consistently positive after a period of this type of discipline or, as I call it, decompression time.

Action Step 3
Boost your brainpower and feed your intelligence

Commit yourself to a continual learning program. The fact that you are reading this book is a clear indication that you are willing to improve yourself through the power of reading. Although this is a huge step toward your ongoing learning program, consider other forms of learning as well. Program yourself to dig for lessons in other arenas, such as the messages you receive in high-quality movies.

Take a closer look at the inadvertent lessons that come from the relationships you maintain. How about looking at the wisdom that can be obtained from your mastermind alliance? Consider forming relationships with healthy elderly folks who are willing to share their considerable experience. Would you consider taking the time to learn about cultures other than your own? All of these aforementioned examples and many more, can stimulate your brainpower and offer maximum growth of your intelligence.

Action Step 4
Shape a unique signature and shape others' perceptions of you

You can dramatically shape the perception others have of you by creating a consistent and positive signature. As we discussed earlier, your signature is the style of behavior you become known for. The signature dynamic operates whether you embrace it or not. If you are not taking the time to plan and direct your actions toward developing a positive signature, you could be running the risk of developing a poor one. Don't fall asleep at the wheel with regard to your signature. Wake up and focus on your personal signature in order to increase your opportunities in life.

"How you do anything, is how you do everything."

- Unknown

Vow to do everything well. Whatever you choose to get involved in, apply a high standard to the endeavor. If you are bussing tables for a living, vow to become the very best bus help at the establishment. If you are in a customer-service industry, vow to care about your customers first before launching a customer-service initiative. If you are dressing professionally, dress for the job you want, not the one you have. Recall the old saying, "How you do anything, is how you do everything." This applies here.

Don't be afraid to develop a little charisma along the way. People will come to know you for your signature and it just may be the interview, before the interview. Oftentimes, the best opportunities come to those who have been highly recommended and your signature can make the strong impression that gains you the positive endorsement. Simply said, your signature can leave others feeling good about you.

Action Step 5
Organize and plan, including time management

Evaluate the systems you currently use for organizing your personal and professional endeavors. Determine if your time-management plan is efficient. Review the amount of time you spend planning your world. Take swift action now to make the changes necessary to dramatically improve in any or all of the above areas. Review the points discussed in this chapter and either seek the help you need to launch your own lifestyle portfolio, or design your own. Combine your development efforts with the time you spend planning your life and you will improve your quality of life in the process.

Summary Points
The Third Essential Law of Life
The Law of Personal and Professional Development

1. Maintain a positive mental attitude with meditation, affirmations, visualization and decompression time

2. Know yourself and remain open to change - raise your deserve level

3. Boost your intelligence with the books you read and people you meet

4. Develop a positive and charismatic personal signature

5. Develop good organizational, time-management and planning skills

Affirmations
Moments for Reflection

1. I spend a minimum of fifteen minutes per day in meditation

2. I know myself intimately; I have earned and deserve abundance in my life

3. I develop excellent relationships with those of diverse backgrounds

4. I read a minimum of one hour each day in respect to my reading program

5. My personal signature is manifesting now and my charisma shines

6. I am an excellent planner. I choose my desired life style prudently

Chapter 7

The Fourth Essential Law of Life
The Law of Accumulation

The Law of Accumulation says that your goals must be measured in bites. That is, set realistic goals that lead up to big goals. Everything counts - minutes, hours, days, weeks - it all adds up. Everything that you do moves you closer to, or further away from, your goals. Many may argue that in order to be a big success, you have to earn big achievements. However, the Law of Accumulation says you only have to be a little bit better in order to be eligible to receive the highest rewards. When all of your small successes add up, they turn into major accomplishments. Focusing on small continual improvements will always leave you feeling good!

How many times in the past have you performed some so-called menial task for someone and the gratitude you received seemed overboard based on your effort? I have discovered that doing little thoughtful things for others often brings affectionate appreciation. Not only do the little things add up in the minds of others but, through the Law of Accumulation, they build up into a steady progression of improvement. If you aim to leave others feeling good, practicing the Law of Accumulation is sure to be a hit.

Consider a few analogies of little advancements and the big rewards associated with the effort. Think of a horse that wins the Triple Crown by a nose. Is he so much better than the horse that comes in second, or is he just a nose better? Literally hundreds of thousands of dollars and, depending on the race, maybe millions of dollars in prize money separate that horse from the horse that came in second. Imagine the feelings of the owners of the horse who loses by a nose in the Triple Crown. Could this be reflective of the Law of Accumulation?

What additional steps could they have taken to be just two noses faster?

Mary Lou Retton - just a little bit better than the competition

How about Mary Lou Retton, who became the first American woman to win an Olympic gold medal in gymnastics in 1984? Did you know her final score was only fifty-thousandths of a point better than that of her second-place competitor? That infinitesimal margin of victory separates her from the nearest contender. She scored perfect tens in the floor and vault routines to clinch the all-around victory. Retton catapulted to international fame at the 1984 Olympics in Los Angeles and her five medals were the most medals won by any athlete at the 1984 Games.

She went on to fame and fortune for being just a little bit better than her competition. Since then, she has garnered national endorsements. She has become a motivational speaker working with major corporations such as Wal-Mart, IBM, General Mills and more. She has had the honor of sharing the center stage with celebrities and dignitaries, from President Ronald Reagan and President Gorbachev to Arnold Schwarzenegger and Michael Jordan. Would you believe she credits much of her success to her commitment to persevere? Retton would say that she was not born with any special gift. Her training regimen required the discipline to get better a little bit at a time, while enduring hardships such as aches and pains and sacrifices. She had no free time and suffered bouts of loneliness stemming from not being able to participate in the kinds of things most other kids her age were doing.

Retton understood the Law of Accumulation very well when she endured the abrasiveness of a tough coach, Bela Karolyi and vowed that no matter how bad it got, she would keep right on going. I agree with Retton when she says it requires no unique talent or special skills to persevere. Success can be attained with stubbornness about accepting nothing less than continual improvement. Winning by getting better a little bit at a time is the best hallmark of the Law of Accumulation! How does this concept leave you feeling?

By the way, do you even remember who came in second at the 1984 Olympics? You will find the answer below in the scores of Retton and her nearest competitor for the women's all-around gymnast:

1st Place - Mary Lou Retton 79.175 - USA
2nd Place - Ecaterina Szabo 79.125 - Romania

Do you recall any pictures on the box of Wheaties for the person who came in second? Are there any million-dollar commercials filmed with the person who came in second? No! Retton did all the things that made her just a little bit better than her competition during the Olympics. And her greatness can be found in perseverance and the Law of Accumulation. Understanding her story and what drove her to the pinnacle of success in the gym and in life is motivating. She left millions of people feeling good about her and her achievements - and I mean by more than just a little bit!

Lance Armstrong - the ambassador of the Law of Accumulation

While we are on the subject of champions, how does the incredible and inspiring story of Lance Armstrong and his fight against cancer leave you feeling? Did I forget to mention his seven straight Tour de France cycling championships? "NEVER BEEN DONE BEFORE!" Armstrong has won more victories in the grueling mental and physical world of competitive cycling than any other athlete. Would you believe all of this came after he was diagnosed with cancer? Believe it, because it is true. Among many things that drove his winner's attitude, one key weapon must be noted: as with Retton, it is perseverance against all odds. Armstrong was an obvious believer in the Law of Accumulation, because that is how he fought to sustain life and to deal with his cancer.

Let's take a trip back in time to understand just how powerful his belief system had to be in order to preserve his world-class winner's spirit. In 1996, at the age of twenty-five, Armstrong was told that he had a very aggressive form of testicular cancer that had also spread to his lungs and brain. If this news wasn't devastating enough, he was diagnosed with a 40-percent chance of survival. This news was a heavy blow to a man who had mapped out a phenomenal career in competitive cycling.

Armstrong could have thrown in the towel at this point and no one would have blamed him. He could have quit. But instead, he set his mind on becoming a world champion and the only thing left to do was fight and beat this cancer by finding the best doctors and trainers available. He continued to work hard to keep his mind positive and focused on the fight of his life. Armstrong endured the dreadful pain of chemotherapy and continued to envision his rehabilitation and return to competitive cycling. Every moment counted, every minute, every hour, every day...

Understanding the Law of Accumulation, mustering a strong will to believe in himself and exercising the power of perseverance made all the difference to his success. This strong will and determination is just about the only thing that could have propelled this unlikely figure into super-stardom. He won his first Tour de France world championship just three years after being diagnosed with cancer. Armstrong, like Retton, has left his mark in the hearts of millions of people. He led the charge in the Law of Accumulation by busting down obstacles, one challenge at a time.

Armstrong is the poster child for the Law of Accumulation. His life continues to demonstrate kindness and incredible courage and charity. He set up the Lance Armstrong Foundation for Testicular Cancer. His dream is to have this charity generate millions of dollars and spread this gift to combat all types of cancer. I can bet I know how his efforts to honor the Law of Accumulation have left you feeling! Great!

The Law of Accumulation can bring life to your efforts

The Law of Accumulation can bring life to your efforts when practiced with sincerity and diligence. I experienced the gift of life when I spent hours, days and weeks nursing the shattered mind of a favorite client back to health. Years ago, one of my clients found himself on the wrong side of a long-term marriage that left him without contact with his four children and abandoned by all of his friends.

I always form personal friendships with my clients, as this helps the relationship develop on several levels. I call this "parallel relationship building." This is when you have more than one relationship with someone and it is allowed to grow on its own path, not affecting other existing relationships you may have with the same person. I have multiple parallel relationships with many of my clients. Those relationships take on the shapes of personal friend, marketing client, life-coaching client, business partner and so on. We exercise whatever relationship is needed based on our mutual concerns.

I was surprised when a client informed me that he felt I was the only friend he had left in the world, because all of his friends had left him and maintained their friendships with his former wife. His world was tumbling down. Based on the macho male-dominated culture he grew up in, it was unheard of to lose all of his friends at once. To lose them to his wife made it even more demoralizing.

The settlement of the divorce forced the closing of his business and left him with no way to pay court-ordered child support or to feed himself. My friend and client became very depressed and suicidal. Each of his phone calls was darker than the last. I found myself on a suicide alert to assist his spirit to keep trying just one more day.

The only thing I thought would help my friend and client was the Law of Accumulation, my theory of nursing him back to positive mental health one minute, one hour and one day at a time. I had no guarantee that our daily conversations would be enough to assuage his heavy grief and dark depression, but I vowed to stay in the fight with him.

The cumulative effects of a caring voice at a critical time paid off. There were more than a handful of times when I was faced with talking the .38 revolver out of the mouth of my friend and client. Each conversation meant either the saving of his life or the failure to connect with him. I was afraid that each call might be our last.

In the years following these dark months, my friend and client would credit me with saving his life. I refused to take credit for such an awesome feat. The credit belonged to him for reaching up through the depression and wanting to live badly enough to carry on. He has rebuilt his world in a marvelous fashion and now has a new set of friends, a new wife and much to live for. He sent me a framed autographed photo of Tiger Woods to express his gratitude for what he recalls as my saving his life. I doubt we will ever rehash those old conversations.

I was overwhelmed by his gesture, but the credit truly

belongs to my understanding of the Law of Accumulation and having the ability to share it with my friend and client to the degree that he got it! Being involved in his life during this period was very exhausting; but in the end, I'm happy to share how it left me feeling. In just one word, I was gratified!

The Law of Accumulation supports the learning process

There are many areas in life where the Law of Accumulation can help us feel better about our pursuits. Among the more common areas where this law takes root is that of learning. I learned some fascinating statistics supporting this. Did you know that if you read just one hour per day in your field and took good notes, in three years you'd be an authority, in five years a national expert and in seven years an international expert? Using the Law of Accumulation by getting better a little bit at a time, consider the reading schedule below:

1 hour per day = 1 book per week
1 book per week = approximately 50 books per year
50 books per year = 500 books over the next 10 years!

The average American reads less than one nonfiction book per year. Reading books helps your personal and professional growth. Reading fifty books per year puts you in the top 1 percent and accelerates your success potential exponentially!

At one point the Gallop Poll survey said the top 1,500 most successful people in the US read 19 books in a year (12 nonfiction and 7 fiction). Imagine where you might be if you followed the theory of reading one hour per day. Imagine the journey of success that might unfold as your outer life changes at a dramatic rate through the positive conditioning of reading just one hour per day!

The American Auto Association studies show that we

drive 12,000 to 25,000 miles per year, which is equivalent to 500 to 1,000 hours per year spent sitting in the car. This is equal to 12.5 to 25 weeks per year or three to six months off every year. This time could be spent learning and growing. This translates into one to two college semesters if we listen to audio books rather than the radio while we drive around. We should invest no less than 5 percent of our annual income in our personal development and we would never have to worry about money.

The Law of Accumulation as it relates to continual learning supports the effort of placing yourself in a position of always getting ready. What are you getting ready for right now? If you can't answer this question instantly, you should consider spending whatever time it takes to come up with an answer. We should always remain in a constant state of getting ready.

As adults, we forget about the steps that prepared us for adulthood. In your early years you remained in a constant state of getting ready. When you were in primary school you were preparing for elementary school. As you were going through elementary school you were preparing for junior high school. High school prepared you for college. Some of us go onto higher education within the college or technical training world, but following this, many of us quit the cycle of getting ready, well before higher education kicks in.

Remaining in a constant state of getting ready is synonymous with practicing the Law of Accumulation and continual learning. The quality of life you build when observing the Law of Accumulation will keep you strong and vibrant for a lifetime.

Can you think of those times where you have violated the Law of Accumulation by giving up too soon or by not staying the course? We live in a world where we expect immediate gratification and this leads to bailing out early if the desired effect doesn't come quickly. How many cycling world championships would Armstrong have won if he quit the moment he was diagnosed with cancer? How about Retton? Would she have won any gold medals in the Olympics if she had quit when she broke her finger or cut her mouth before the 1984 Olympic Games? Would Retton or Armstrong have gone onto great fortune and fame without remaining in a constant state of getting ready while respecting the Law of Accumulation?

Think about the times in your life when the Law of Accumulation could have worked positively for you on your way to achieving your goals and aspirations, if you had stayed with the plan. You must persevere long after others quit - it's like the Longfellow verse that says, "Those heights by great men won and kept, were not achieved by sudden flight, but they while their companions slept…were toiling upwards in the night." Your perseverance must burn like a white-hot fire!

The white-hot burning desire theory!

It is imperative that you have a white-hot burning desire for success; you will be far more likely to take the necessary actions to bring the essential laws of life into your world.

There is a parable about Socrates, the philosopher and a young man who desperately sought out wisdom. The parable paints a vivid picture of desire:

A young man approached Socrates and said to him, "Socrates you are the wisest man in the land; how do I learn to be as wise as you are?" Before answering the question, Socrates asked the young man to take a walk with him and they strolled to a nearby lake. The two of them walked into the lake until it was about waist high. Socrates suddenly grabbed the young man by the neck and aggressively dunked his head under the water.

"Those heights by great men won and kept, were not achieved by sudden flight, but they while their companions slept… were toiling upwards in the night."

- Longfellow

At first the young man didn't struggle, as he thought Socrates was just joking.

After a short time the young man began to struggle and wriggle around trying to surface for air. Socrates still held him under the water and just before the young man's lungs began to burn for lack of oxygen, Socrates released him and the young man sprung up into the air. He was gasping and spurting for air. Socrates looked at the young man and said, "When you desire knowledge, with the same intensity as you desire to breathe, then nothing can stop you from getting it." How do you think this tough lesson on desire and wisdom left the young man feeling? Now that is a picture of white-hot burning desire!

Remember this parable and the white-hot burning desire to breathe air the next time someone holds your proverbial head underwater against your will. This parable is a metaphor for motivation - the white-hot burning desire - on the path to success!

Key Action Steps
The Law of Accumulation

Action Step 1
Improve by a little bit

After you have created a life plan and established your goals, go back to the plan. Break it down into smaller objectives before executing it. Improve each critical area by a little bit each day. You will attain all of your major goals in this way.

Action Step 2
Consider the competition

As you work on projects to improve the quality of your life and the lives of others through the Law of Accumulation, consider your competition. How much better do you really need to be over your closest competitor? In order to become a consistent winner in life, you don't have to be that much better than your competition. Most people will not go that little extra step in life. When you take small additional steps in life, it brings you out in front of your closest competitor.

Action Step 3
Can this theory of a little bit be this easy?

The theory of becoming a little bit better and the Law of Accumulation truly is an easy concept both to grasp and to do. It merely takes initiative, discipline and will-power. Everything falls into place when you combine these three simple ingredients. It is just that easy.

Action Step 4
Never throw in the towel

A real winner never throws in the towel. Never, never, never quit. Set your mind on your goal. Determine what it will take to achieve it and then do a little bit more along the way. Develop a winner's mentality. Work very hard to keep your mind focused and strong during your endeavors toward goal attainment. Build a strong support network as you strengthen your belief in yourself and your abilities. Remain steadfast regarding how you do things. Never throw in the towel.

Action Step 5
Build multiple parallel relationships

Make every effort to get the most from your relationships. Form multiple parallel relationships whenever possible. The beauty of these relationships is that they allow you to compress time and build more layers toward life fulfillment. You may be able to switch from one aspect of a relationship to another, within a few key relationships. The concept of building multiple parallel relationships within your chosen circle will prove to be very rewarding.

Summary Points
The Fourth Essential Law of Life
The Law of Accumulation

1. Break down your big goals into measurable bite-sized objectives

2. Everything that you do either moves you closer to, or further away from, your goals

3. Develop a white-hot burning desire for success on your life journey

4. The Law of Accumulation moves mountains with persistence

5. Continue to improve and to reach your goals by becoming a little bit better

Affirmations
Moments for Reflection

1. I build multiple parallel relationships within my inner circle of influence

2. I live my life from the perspective of a winner's attitude

3. I break large goals down into small bite-size objectives

4. I live and breathe the Law of Accumulation

5. I make every minute, of every hour, of every day, count

Chapter 8

The Fifth Essential Law of Life
The Law of Attraction

There are many perspectives to the Law of Attraction. As you have discovered in previous chapters, other essential laws of life have blended quite well with one another, producing dynamic synergies. The Law of Attraction is no different and works closely with the other essential laws.

The Law of Attraction is a powerful law and, when fully understood, will create a life of abundance. This law is as much about what you give away as about what you receive in the process. The following accounts will serve to be reaffirming and will add a dynamic to your life that may help you discover how to attract the things you want and need.

How you leave others feeling impacts the quality of people you attract

Do you hate people? What are the worst ways you can think of to leave others feeling? How do others leave you feeling? Many of us seldom take the time to ponder how we leave others feeling and how this affects the type of people we attract to us.

Are you happy with the people you currently have surrounding you in your life? Who are the people you work closely with? What are the typical characteristics of those you call a friend? Is your significant other someone that you are proud of and feel appropriately matched up with?

If you have not answered positively to the majority of these questions, then it is time to take a look at the choices you have made and why you may be inadvertently attracting people to you who are not good for you. Consider this additional question: Could the people you surround yourself with have toxic personalities? You may be very surprised to learn this and a good measure of "house cleaning" may be in order to rid yourself of toxic people and unhealthy circumstances.

A reality check - are you attracting the wrong people or circumstances?

A reality check is the answer to the question of why you may be attracting the wrong people or circumstances into your life. Let's examine what it takes to be on the right side of this fifth essential law of life. Are you outgoing? Do you extend help to strangers and friends alike? Are you likely to say please and thank you during your everyday interactions? The best people are attracted to those who have personal charm, charisma or a high likeability factor. There is one supreme reason for this: how you leave them feeling!

Many times you must give up - to go up. In other words, you must be willing to give up energy, time and resources to others in order to build the type of charisma others are attracted to. The phenomenal thing about this law is that the more you attract things, people and circumstances into your life, the greater the chances of having the same things, people and circumstances be attracted to you. You can control the floodgates of good tidings by becoming cognizant and respectful of both your ability to attract good people and quality circumstances and your basic understanding of the power of this attraction.

Being attractive supports the Law of Attraction

Although unfair, the fortune of being born attractive plays right into the gifts of the Law of Attraction. Our world is far more giving to attractive people than to unattractive people. It is not a subject matter that is talked about much at parties or even around the board-room, but it is very true.

How many unattractive women do you see gracing the covers of Cosmopolitan or Playboy? The male counter-part is no different. Can you recall unattractive men splashed across a G.Q. Magazine? When was the last time some unattractive retail peddler flashed across your TV screen in an attempt to persuade you to buy some product?

Even celebrity endorsements rely heavily on the most attractive celebrities to push their products. Figures like Michael Jordan, Tiger Woods, Anna Kornikova and Andre Agassi endorse products that range from under-wear to fancy cars and high-fashion clothing. Com-panies don't shell out millions of dollars in product endorsements to unattractive celebrities.

Although a professional tennis player, there was a time when Anna Kornikova was making far more money on the endorsement payroll than by playing tennis; she hadn't even won a major tournament. The Law of Attraction brings big rewards to attractive people. It may not be fair or pleasant, but it is very true. If this leaves you feeling badly, you may ask: What can I do about not being blessed with beauty? I say plenty!

Make yourself attractive from the inside and this increases your attractiveness on the outside. Beauty is not always what we can see with our eyes; sometimes it is what we feel with our hearts. When an attractive per-sonality arrives to light up the room, we are attracted, regardless of their physical imperfections. Someone who possesses inner beauty without the fortune of outer beauty may never grace the cover of any famous beauty magazine, but they will always leave a favorable impres-sion on you. Infectious personality types have a way of leaving footprints in your heart. We detailed this theory of leaving your signature behind and footprints in the hearts of others in Chapter 2. The point is worth repeating here, as it is a key way to balance the scales of justice by improving areas of your character. This can accelerate the Law of Attraction in your life.

Can your upbringing affect the Law of Attraction?

How much influence does the manner in which you were raised have on the choices you make in life? Have you ever asked yourself this question, "Does the quality of my choices have anything to do with how I was raised?" Does your early upbringing affect who you are? Can you overcome familial and situational wrongs? Know this: Our family experience always has an effect on what type of adults we become and this shapes the quality of choices and decisions we make in life.

Most people set the boundaries of their choices and restricted their decisions based on what they know. Oftentimes, they don't know what they don't know. This is primarily because of family upbringing and self-imposed limitations! You don't have to experience an epiphany in order to stimulate the Law of Attraction and make it work for you. Simply possessing the desire to increase your exposure to a broad range of positive influences will increase your learning opportunities. The more learning opportunities you have, the stronger the Law of Attraction. This perpetuates positive growth and leaves you feeling good. Your family experience is thus important, but it is not the ultimate determinant of your destiny.

The theories of abundance and scarcity impact the Law of Attraction

Have you every asked yourself why some people have a lot of money while others live their lives penniless? Material means are not the primary measures of the Law of Attraction. However, please note the universal Law of Money works with the Law of Attraction. The theories of abundance and scarcity play positive and negative roles in this hypothesis.

As you embrace a mindset of abundance, your subconscious mind finds a way to manifest your beliefs. This is the positive perspective. On the other hand, a mindset of fearfulness and feelings of financial peril lock into the mindset of scarcity. Your subconscious mind goes to work just as hard on helping you destroy, throw away or give away fortune and opportunities in order to fulfill your scarcity mentality. This portion of the theory plays the role of the "evil twin" and is clearly negative. Understanding the theories of abundance and scarcity will place you in the driver's seat when it comes to choosing the quality of life you want to attract.

In the past I noticed that whenever I found myself in a situation in which I had no money, the pipeline to cash had seemed to dry up. Experience and maturity, however, taught me that it was my own self-imposed fear and feelings of scarcity that kept me broke. Conversely, when I made the mental adjustment to thoughts of abundance I was compelled to take positive action. I began saving small amounts of money. The Law of Attraction worked like a lucky charm because more money and avenues for generating cash came to me like a powerful energy.

I believe money has energy and in order to attract money to you, you must respect both the Law of Money and the Law of Attraction. This understanding has to be followed by a strong belief in the theory of abundance. Other key ways to help the energy of money move in your favor is to value yourself by always paying yourself first, before you pay anyone else. Initially you may start with small amounts, but keep them consistent and increase the amounts the instant you are able to.

The other principle is that you must share your fortune by helping others who are less fortunate. Prudently giving money away to worthy causes makes the Law of Attraction go into extreme overdrive. The rewards are limitless! I believe those who are allowed to earn or come into contact with large sums of money are merely custodians of that money. You are intended to help others while helping yourself when you are blessed with the gift of financial freedom. You will continue to attract money to you when you understand and respect the power and energy of money and the universal law of giving. The Law of Attraction will discontinue the accumulation of fortune if you become too selfish and start hoarding money for your sole use.

A key to understanding the Law of Attraction as it relates to money has to do with wasteful over-consumption. It includes buying goods that are purchased and go unused. You are disrespecting the privilege of being financially free when you become an over-consumer.

Whenever you live with disrespect, you cause the Law of Attraction to block growth. If you find yourself spending your cash on items which you rarely or never use, this is wasteful and disrespectful. It causes clutter and clutter creates havoc. Your mind becomes cluttered with the thought of where to put all of the items that you cannot use. This doesn't leave you feeling good.

The best way to release yourself from the grips of wasteful spending is to launch a plan to buy more of the things you need and less of the things you merely want. Also, you must simplify your life by giving away the items that you have not used for an extended period of time. Find others who will be helped through the gift of the item, which may have plenty of life and value still in it. Through the Law of Attraction, this gift is recognized and other items that serve you best are ushered into your life. Know that a gesture such as this leaves both you and the recipient of your gift feeling good!

Key Action Steps
The Law of Attraction

Action Step 1
Create a life of abundance

Study the Law of Attraction in order to cultivate momentum in your life. Set your goals commensurate with living a life of abundance as you include the Law of Attraction in your life model.

Action Step 2
Take stock of the people you are attracting

Take the time to periodically take stock of the people you are attracting. Remain flexible and willing to make the changes needed in order to attract the right people, situations and energy into your life.

Action Step 3
Be attractive; it supports your cause

Being someone who maintains a positive and attractive presence will help you bring people into your life whom you want to serve. In turn, they will want to serve you. Take the necessary time to make yourself attractive; you will feel better.

Action Step 4
Heal family influences

If you had a challenging family upbringing, don't let this hold you back. Take special care to obtain the help you need to remove family roadblocks from your psyche. This single move will help jump-start your engine of motivation.

Action Step 5
Harness the power of the subconscious mind

Point your subconscious mind in the right direction toward living the life you deserve. Positive thoughts (which are like proper rest and nourishment to your mind) serve your needs without fail. The more positive you become, the more the Law of Attraction kicks in.

Summary Points
The Fifth Essential Law of Life
The Law of Attraction

1. How you leave others feeling impacts on the quality of the people you attract

2. Grow in your ability to attract the best people by extending yourself to others

3. Strive to achieve beauty and balance both on the inside and outside

4. Don't let family shackles hold you back from success

5. Remove all roadblocks that keep you from attracting positive support

Affirmations
Moments for Reflection

1. I feed my brain with mentally stimulating beliefs and ideas

2. I believe in the power of the subconscious mind

3. The Law of Attraction is consistently connecting me with good influences

4. I create a life of abundance from my powerful belief system

5. I am becoming stronger and healthier daily via the Law of Attraction

Chapter 9

Friends and Family: A Global Community - The Village Shines the Light

"It takes a village to raise a child." Do you fully understand what this wonderful expression means? What it means to me is that the family that I was born into is my first family. And about this I had little choice - at least in the physical realm. For many people, this family, while important, is not fully sustaining.

Should you expect to receive your entire diet of "life nourishment" from this first family? Or could one of life's early lessons perhaps be that embracing life force, sustained happiness and exponential development are to be found in the quest for and acquisition of, additional significant influences?

Could the key to those other influences be found in your "second-family" options? I'm currently a member of at least a half a dozen other significant "second" families. In this case, the term second simply means additional significant families, rather than second place behind the first family. The second-family ideal exemplifies the friends and family concept to the fullest.

As noted above, your first family may not offer you the full complement of life nutrients to complete your ultimate mission in life. There are a number of metaphysical teachings that state that we choose which family we are born into. Regardless, the opportunity for alternate significant families exists for those who desire them. They come as a result of planning, passion and perseverance.

Assess your first-family situation and determine if the experience was rich enough to nurture your dreams into reality. This is the time to design your life plan. The best plans start with your acceptance of the power and enrichment of second-family dynamics. The village shines the light!

Rather than harboring resentment and frustration over the things your first family did not, or could not, give you, find a way through the second-family option to persevere toward the brightest light of life. And, rather than waiting for your second-family options to show up at your door step, venture out and endeavor to earn the sustenance they offer. Your passion for self-improvement can only be matched by your perseverance in attaining the gifts that your second families can offer. Passion and perseverance are complements in this endeavor. You could not achieve your maximum development and second-family acquisitions without the teamwork of passion and perseverance - backed by proper planning.

You have a treasure trove of opportunities to develop other family connections along the way. In fact, should you decide to develop other relationships, think big. Continue to peal back multiple layers off the onion of life. At the same time, create maximum diversity in building your extended families. Wherever you are in life, decide to seek and to hold the best second-family relationships imaginable and vow to leave your signature on them.

The paradigm created from this type of forward thinking is the answer to all that you can dream and become! Anyone, without much effort, can become good at what they do or become good in managing life's general skills. However, it takes a very special person to embark upon the road to greatness. Moreover, no one in history has ever become great alone! Julius Caesar had his empire, Jesus Christ had his disciples and Winston Churchill had the love and support of an entire nation and related allies.

All of these great leaders were supported by their village. They created mastermind alliances within the village and were fully supported in their efforts to become great through leadership mastery. These charismatic leaders gleaned light and wisdom from their village and returned that energy back to important others and their societies. The village shines the light!

Who are the members of your village? Is your village moving you toward the light of your destiny? Are confusion, neglect or apathy creating shadows in your path? Or, worse, are you faced with utter darkness as though staring into a mirrored reflection of crude oil? Are you standing still or regressing? If you can't answer positively to these questions, you just may need to let go of your current village!

It has been proven throughout the ages that the village will indeed shore up your life efforts. Take full stock of your station in life and make the necessary changes that will increase your quality of life. Build your winning team by taking the time to elect a new tribal leader and cast out any unwanted villagers in order to make room for a re-elected group. Your growth and synergy depend on the quality of the village. In addition, your destiny is either accelerated or thwarted by the direction and instruction you receive from your village.

Yet another layer peals away from the onion when you consider the notion of being raised by a global village. Why limit your scope to the local and regional areas that we all typically reside in? Push your vision to the outer limits of your life by participating on a world scale and in a global community as a bona fide card-carrying member.

Never allow your membership to be revoked. I learned the concept of staying in the game from one of the greatest thinkers in my village. In fact, this person is a very important member of my second-family network. Frederick C. Elliott states, "In life, once you get in,

*"In life,
once you
get in,
always
keep your
feet at the
bargaining
table."*

- Frederick C. Elliott

always keep your feet at the bargaining table." Although Fred's notion is quite simple, it is sage advice and I follow it to the letter!

I have found exponential growth on my journey to success by way of positive input from my fellow global villagers and mastermind alliance. These second-family associations have been the lifeblood of my continued development. I have also discovered that if you truly leave your signature upon people (I mean a deep indelible mark) you will earn the rights of lifetime membership and the reward of reciprocal relationships. Proof of continual rewarding relationships can be found in the following story.

You can take the boy out of the village

Just one life story can say volumes about persevering in the course of perpetual obstacles and unimaginable injustices. Hurdling roadblocks and systematically breaking down "good old boy" rules of the game were commonplace for the boy in this story.

He was born into a family of eight children during very difficult times. His parents were young and moderately skilled. Although both parents possessed intelligence and "street smarts," their educational endeavors did not go beyond a high school education. To add to their life challenges, the sixties were times of oppression and prejudice. Meanwhile, every life created by the boy's parents came with a mouth to feed. This was coupled with an unquenchable hunger for normalcy, to enjoy life's toys and conveniences.

The parents of this young boy wanted to give him and his brothers and sisters all the things in life they never had. Both parents were from the south. The boy's mother hailed from Louisiana and his father from Mississippi. While the sixties were tough times, growing up in the rural south had been even rougher for the boy's parents.

The main messages taught to this boy and his siblings were kindness to others, respecting self and elders and getting a good education. The parents of the boy, although not perfect, attempted to practice what they preached. They always took in others who seemed to have fallen on hard times. And as long as the boy could remember, there was always a friend of the family living in their home. The belief was that it is noble to lend a hand up, rather than ask for a hand out from others. This was a key message he received from his upbringing. This sense of giving, maintained through adulthood, was one of the crown jewels among the many life lessons that the boy learned from his parents.

The parents of the boy knew they couldn't provide everything for him while he was growing up and they elected to leave the south and settle in northern Nevada. They did this in order to provide a livelihood for the family. This also created a more diverse culture to which to expose their children.

His parents had somehow stumbled upon the second-family philosophy and simultaneously created second-family situations for those in need. His parents also chose a community that, although bearing some injustices, offered exposure to others who might allow second-family options for their children. The boy delighted in the opportunity for happiness and continual development that this new community afforded him. Ultimately he captured just the right nurturing from a smorgasbord full of second-family relationships.

The potpourri of relationships started with his fourth-grade teacher, who showed him kindness and educational outreach beyond the curriculum. This torch of love and care was also shared by his eighth-grade art teacher, who embraced him like no other student.

The boy has grown to his mid-forties and, although the community has long since split up and moved to other places, he remains in close communication with those teachers from the village. The connection is stronger than ever and they have long since evolved to the level of mastermind status. They are an integral part of this man's village.

The gifts of this mastermind alliance are plenty, but the outstanding endowments are no doubt the development of courage, determination and love. Strength was born early through the efforts of this man's fourth-grade teacher, Mrs. Essenpreis. In addition, his eighth-grade art teacher, Mrs. Ludwig Peterson, milled and processed his raw talent into that of a fine artist.

In fact, the full art scholarship to the University of Nevada at Las Vegas would not have been possible without Mrs. Peterson's tireless devotion and special touch! To this day, he still travels periodically for special workshops with his eighth-grade art teacher and creatively splashes out paintings of seascapes and the like. The bond is stronger than ever. Continual and rewarding associations can be found in these significant second-family relationships and this man's story is solid proof of these facts. What seemed like a passing moment through puberty has extended into a lifetime of friendships.

As you consider this unique situation, you are left with the fact that the teachers and the man have truly left their signatures upon one another. A deep indelible mark is evidence of the long-term relationship with the teachers in the man's village. Another blessing is that after nearly forty years, the relationships continue to grow and evolve. This is where the true essence of the village is discovered. It is clear that the boy who is now a man has earned the rights of lifetime membership and continual rewarding and reciprocal relationships with his significant second families. It is also evident that they have positively and dramatically shaped his world; and he has permanently shaped theirs as well.

The village contributes to self-esteem and character-building for all of its members

Let's examine it this way: Just two of the man's many second-family relationships from the village contributed to his core self-esteem and positive disposition. Both villagers and mastermind alliance members, Mrs. Essenpreis and Mrs. Peterson, contributed to the boy's higher education, which led to the attainment of multiple degrees. Common sense, laced with a generous helping of street smarts and a fair accompaniment of book smarts, led to a career of executive-level positions. This of course shifted his lifestyle index upward - leaving him and those around him feeling good.

I am that boy who has grown into manhood and this is my story. I transferred the theory of the village concept and the search for eligible second families to my world beyond the initial village I was raised in. My village made great contributions to my character and self-esteem. As they say, "You can take the boy out of the village, but you can't take the village out of the boy." These principles are universal. The village concept works everywhere.

As I applied my skills to multiple trades, I never forgot the power of the second-family influence. I spread that commitment across my corporate America clients and associates as well. The experience has been rewarding. Working as a marketing executive in Las Vegas and touching literally hundreds and thousands of lives over the past twenty-seven years made the village concept an everlasting principle.

Second-family influence and the handshake theory in action

I launched my professional speaking company, JessTalk Speaking Services, a few years ago on the strength of the second-family network of villagers and mastermind members. I owe a world of gratitude to the village. The many lessons learned have propelled me into a position on the success journey that has the potential of making me a maven of lifestyle and commerce!

I have always believed in the theory that we are only one handshake away from an entirely different and uplifting lifestyle. This theory was put to the test when I shook the hand of one of my greatest clients thus far, Derek Elliott, President and CEO of the EMI Group.

JessTalk currently manages a dozen different relationships with the EMI Group. All of these relationships with Elliott and his company began with a handshake more than seven years ago. As a prelude to its current maturing status, the initial relationship began with an emerging camaraderie and professional relationship. This developed into a strong personal friendship and partnership.

As part of my professional speaking responsibilities, I have been working as a Lifestyles Coach for personal and professional development for Elliott and his chain of companies in the Dominican Republic, Canada and the United States. These relationships have dramatically shifted my lifestyle index to a very healthy place. Derek is a prominent constituent of the village and a distinguished mastermind alliance member. He continues to shine the light from the villager standpoint onto my paradigm of life.

JessTalk Speaking Services has experienced defining moments as a result of that warm light and my relationship with Elliott and his companies. As an example, the moment he saw the JessTalk website years ago, he blurted out: "I want to be your largest customer." He made this statement before he had a chance to read the content of the website. This immediate statement was made by Elliott as a direct result of his faith in my abilities. It was what I might call residual strength gained from my previous occupation.

The following observation by Elliott says it best: "Each may have their own definition of success. However, there are common qualities that define leaders. Jesse is a true leader in the sense that he lives his life according to his life strategies and philosophies. He walks the talk. The integrity, listening ability and organizational skills that Jesse has brought to me personally, as well as to our companies, have allowed us to move forward at new speeds that are required for advanced success in today's world."

At the point of this writing, the EMI Group indeed remains the largest JessTalk client. JessTalk Speaking Services was launched into the world of global communications serving international addresses at the insistence of Elliott and the EMI Group. We have multiple contracts with their holdings in Toronto and Orangeville, Canada; the Dominican Republic; and the United States. This momentum has spread to additional opportunities for JessTalk to serve other international companies, located in Vancouver, Canada. I believe the Law of Attraction is helping to grow the international team of villagers.

The EMI Group supports JessTalk by hiring our services for keynote addresses at their VIP conferences, speaking tours and JessTalk lifestyles coaching for their senior and vice president-level executives.

We have also formed additional companies together - most notably, Elliott Motion Pictures, where I serve as Vice President of the company. Elliott Motion Pictures has currently produced two major Hollywood films in conjunction with our industry partners, Media 8, lead by Stewart Hall and Sammy Lee out of Los Angeles and Hong Kong, respectively. We will no doubt have secured our third motion picture deal by the time this book is released.

We enjoy creating companies that help improve the quality of life for others. We use a system that I call the Quantum Strength Pillars to measure our success. In our world, a pillar is a business or infrastructure that participates in commerce and produces revenues for our companies. Quantum Strength Pillars are those infra-structures that help us take a quantum leap in our efforts to help others, while enjoying reciprocal effects from our endeavors.

JessTalk clients enjoy the awareness retreat tours. These tours are one of the special relationship vehicles that Elliott and I enjoy. The first international tour was launched in his honor. We embarked on the journey of moving commando style through parts of the United States, Europe and Canada. This international version of the D.J. Tours was created in order to remove both the client and coach from familiar environments.

We discovered that leaving our respective environ-ments caused us to think quite differently. This was as a result of being exposed to different smells, languages, environments and cultures. We started in Toronto, Canada and flew directly to Paris, France. We then moved by train to Geneva, Switzerland and on to Cannes and St. Tropez by car. This eye-opening expe-rience then took us to Naples, Capri and Ana Capri. Finally, we settled in Rome for the last four days of our sixteen-day journey.

I would call this experience a "vision stretcher." Both Elliott and I continued to open our respective global offices while pushing the bar on our coaching/client relationship. We emerged from that journey as much different men than when we began it. Our minds were far more open and our individual mind-body-spirit balance was vibrant and fresh. I remain appreciative and grateful that Elliott, his family and associated companies are all part of my global village community and second-family circle.

If you are looking to harness the power of the friends and family connection along the lines I have described here - I say, go for it. You will never regret your endeavor. Additional benefits abound. I have gained great strength and definite purpose through my exposure to Elliott and others like him. I continue to enjoy the warmth from the light shone by the village.

As I noted earlier, the one handshake away from an entirely different lifestyle theory represents truth and positive thinking. Elliott has proven this theory by backing up his handshake with actions. This handshake extends from his father Frederick C. Elliott to his brother Drew, sister-in-law Melanie, stepfather Joe and mother Betty Elliott-Kichler.

I have found great strength in numbers. You get the full-package deal with this family and they hit you from a different angle with each of their varied personalities when you are connecting with them. You, too, can create second-family dynamics and synergistic realities by fully embracing the concept of how you leave them feeling!

I'm happy to note that I learned the power of the second family long before I needed to test out any other theory. Whenever I think about how healthy my personal and professional relationships are with the Elliott and Kichler families, the one common thread that remains deep and true is their appreciation of how I continue to leave them feeling!

Passively earning influence

Adherence to the how you leave them feeling concept results in a conscious and conscientious effort to maintain the freshest, brightest, most inviting attitude and demeanor. It works much like the power of your subconscious mind. When you practice the power of how you leave them feeling and hone this philosophy to a tool of exquisite precision, it works effortlessly, much like a rhythmically moving windmill on a soft breezy summer day.

Are you familiar with the concept of passive income? I think of passive income much like "stay-at-home money." You don't have to leave home to earn it - it works for you while you simply stay at home. Passive income or stay-at-home money is the money you earn through the power of compounding interest, through your investments. Your earning potential is realized without having to put forth any sweat-labor to earn it.

Passive influence is much like passive income. The best way to earn passive influence (which can lead to affluence) is by making lasting connections in your global village. And the best way to build those connections is to focus your energies on building your character and your mindset. The ultimate goal is to own a charismatic personality. The charisma that you cultivate will put you in the driver's seat of life. You will continue to prosper via the building of privileged relationships as a direct reflection of the power of your charisma.

This alone will turn on the power of the Law of Attraction and the right people will begin showing up in your life to help you fulfill your destiny. Challenge yourself to live the life you deserve. Your determination to accept the responsibility of how you leave them feeling will serve you well.

How you leave them feeling and your personal trademark in the village

Buying into the powers and theories of how you leave them feeling is like subscribing to an exclusive membership. It is often said: "Membership has its privileges!" This is true in the world of how you leave them feeling as well.

It is rather ironic that even in today's global village of mass communication, the concept and potential rewards of how you leave them feeling seem to be a well-kept secret. Very few people thus subscribe to the theory and even fewer put it into practice. But just imagine: What kind of life could you create for yourself and your family if, every day, you practiced the simple theory of how you leave them feeling?

The Law of Accumulation serves you well in this instance. What if you continued working on the goal of attaining a charismatic personality to the degree that your finest mannerisms acquired the distinction of a trademark? What if your personal style of relating to people took on the power of a well-known brand name?

Would this positively change your life? You bet it would! There would be legions of supporters modeling and spreading your best traits as a result of appreciating how you leave them feeling. Do you recall the axiom that imitation is the highest form of flattery? Once you get the members in your village to connect to your unique style - your personal brand of interaction - who knows where the results would take you?

I'm sure that way back in 1906 when the Haloid Company was founded, its founders had not considered that around 1960, Chester F. Carlson would create and license a process called Xerography. This new process was so good that Xerox became a household brand name that, today, we all know very well. How many times have you heard someone say, "Hey, go and Xerox this for me?" Or perhaps you have heard others walk into an office supply store and ask the clerk, "How much are your Xerox copies?" There may not actually be any Xerox machines in the store; the actual machines might be Hewlett-Packard or IBM. The inquirer obviously intended to ask about photocopying services. I can't remember the last time I heard someone refer to photocopying over Xeroxing.

What about when you ask someone to hand you a Kleenex? Is it Kleenex you are really looking for, or is it tissue? The branding of Kleenex is so strong that it has found its way into our everyday communication and virtually replaced the generic product called tissue. Who would have thought back in 1872, when the Kimberly-Clark Company was first established, that it would create a brand that became the catchword for a popular item such as tissue? It is no surprise that Kimberly-Clark has been able to reach annual revenues of over $15 billion dollars with Kleenex and other products.

To conclude the examples of the power of brand awareness, let's consider one well-known human case in point. The many watchers of classic comedy reruns will recall the trademark words made famous by a brilliant comedic team. "Heeeeeeeeeere's Johnny!" This is, of course, the voice of Ed McMahon announcing the charismatic Johnny Carson. Carson was the icon of late night television and the Tonight Show. His unique style of humor and personality included great timing, charm, devilish personality, angelic charisma and more class than you will find in a schoolroom.

Carson spent three decades with NBC and The Tonight Show. It was his witty and amusing reactions to people and circumstances that polished his distinct brand of performing and of interacting with guests and audiences. There have been countless facsimiles of Carson's style since his departure. Everyone from Jay Leno to David Letterman owes their wealth and celebrity to the model Carson created. He had an innate ability for knowing how his audiences would respond to his antics and his sense of humor never let up. Carson was a master at the concept of how you leave them feeling. He tickled our funny bone and left us feeling great!

Okay, so maybe the distinctiveness of your personal traits doesn't make it to Kleenex or Xerox status, but could you envision changing the lives of others with your brand-worthy personality? Perhaps you do not want to strive for work on a television sound stage or climb to the heights of Carson. But can you envision the power of creating a unique personal brand of relating to people within your own village?

Do you know the number of lives, including your own, that can shift upward as a result? This is the concept of personal branding - that is, a signature way of behaving that may be shared within your own village, to the mutual benefit of all concerned. As you embark upon this approach, take the time to get a feel for what is important to others as well as to yourself. Make every effort to ascertain where people are coming from as you engage in interpersonal communication. The good that follows such a quest is hard to quantify. Our first essential law of life, the Law of Attitude is alive and well within the idea of personal branding.

Second-family stories and the power of personal branding

As I consider examples of personal branding, there are a number of stories that I could share with you, but none more special than the continuing story of my relationship with Charles and Norma Meeks in the global village. This couple has been instrumental in shining the light of commitment and excellence on me. They are second-family and mastermind players in my expanding global village.

It is this association that took my level of understanding about the sixth essential law of life, the Law of Cause and Effect, to a much higher level. My seven-year relationship with the Meeks' continues to strengthen daily. I no longer feel amazement at seeing my picture among other family pictures hanging over their fireplace mantle piece. Personal branding is exemplified here in this thoughtful tribute, a signature behavior of this caring couple.

My role in the Meeks family has become vital to many of the important facets of their lives. On the other hand, many of my significant decisions are either shaped by their influence or directly derived from their teachings. The beauty of this relationship is centered in how we leave one another feeling, rather than what we have done for one another. Are there families that you have an opportunity to touch and develop second-family ties with? Will you take the necessary action to forge those relationships right now?

If you answer yes to these questions, strap yourself in and prepare for positive life-changing situations. If you answer no to the question of whether you have second-family relationships that are ripe for developing, you seriously need to search your heart and answer a deeper question: "Why not?" This is your chance to improve the quality of your life. There is no better time to place the magnifying glass over pivotal points of your character. Do this in order to develop to your fullest potential.

"Poor is the man who knows what he is going to eat at the end of the day."

- Vittorio Ciccone

Vittorio Ciccone states that, "Poor is the man who knows what he is going to eat at the end of the day." I learned this powerful lesson, which was passed on to help me through a difficult professional transition. There are many connotations to this quote. The most compelling message I get from it is to take ownership of my destiny - a destiny of improving constantly, rather than just knowing and accepting, what is possible for today. This applies whether you are a schoolteacher constantly pushing the envelope of your style of education or a police officer looking to serve his community. Always go the extra mile to improve yourself and others. Refuse to sit back and accept only what others may throw your way. Strengthen your spirit by helping yourself when looking for help from others.

This is the wisdom I gained from Vittorio Ciccone, who is yet another member of my village - my global community. He emigrated from southern Italy and this Italian Canadian embodies the best in human spirit. Ciccone wrote the book on how you leave them feeling long before the concept became a part of my vision. He and his wife, Palma, run their lives on a few cornerstone beliefs that they brought with them across the waters when they immigrated to Vancouver, Canada, more than 50 years ago.

This proud European could not speak one word of English when he first came to Canada. He has since added English to his repertoire of languages as he has climbed the economic ladder of success. Ciccone attributes his success to one simple belief: "People are always taking your measure." Think about this statement for a moment. What does it mean to you?

"People are always taking your measure."

- Vittorio Ciccone

What it means to me is to take care of how I present myself to the world. Be cognizant of how you dress when you leave your home for any occasion. Consider how you treat strangers, acquaintances, colleagues, friends and family. Put a special emphasis on how you manage your relationships. The more I think about the impact of Ciccone's words, the more I'm reminded that the exact same principles fuel the power of how you leave them feeling! The wisdom in Ciccone's message and the power of how you leave them feeling are synergistic.

Consider that how you leave others feeling, accompanied by people taking your measure, can be a dynamic duo with which to be armed. As you accept both concepts into your world, your life will be significantly enhanced. Recall that this pair of concepts embodies the many messages found in the third essential law of life, the Law of Personal and Professional Development.

The Ciccones practice what they preach. They raised their children on sound principles of success. All of their children are entrepreneurs and make positive contributions to their communities. In fact, this book would largely not be possible if it were not for the support, guidance and strength of Robert Ciccone, their youngest son.

Robert is the President and CEO of Success Unlimited Marketing Group. This applied consulting firm specializes in helping businesses increase their sales and profits (www.susmg.com). Robert serves as a member of my JessTalk Speaking Services board of directors. He also serves as my life coach. His company is responsible for creating the image and marketing strategy for this book and all other JessTalk ventures.

A few years ago, I flew from Las Vegas, Nevada, to Vancouver, Canada, to seek council from Robert and his brother Anthony Ciccone. They closed down their respective offices for three days while they mentored my transition from twenty-seven years of working in corporate America into the fascinating world of entrepreneurship. The support they provided was over the top and my transition would have been next to impossible without their help.

I met Robert and Anthony as a result of developing a personal and professional relationship with Vittorio more than fifteen years ago. If I hadn't had at least a thread of the how you leave them feeling concept running though my veins when I met Vittorio, my future would be entirely different right now. There is clear evidence that the power of the village has benefited me and that this second-family addition has been life altering.

It is important to share a bit of the profile of Robert Ciccone in order to paint the full picture of what drives such a great man. His soul is steeped in strong family values. There is a natural goodness about him. Robert is married to Christina, who also works very closely with him at the Success Unlimited Marketing Group. Like Vittorio, Robert practices what he preaches. He runs his personal life with respect and class. He cares for his family and friends, especially his daughter Alyssa and his wife Christina. He also can't forget the life messages taught by his parents and he shares the benefit of his knowledge with others.

I'm fortunate and appreciative that Robert and Christina are members of my second family and global village. Robert is truly a dedicated member of my village and mastermind group. The friends and family concept takes on a special meaning in my relationship with the Ciccones. They continue to shine a bright spotlight on my success journey!

This chapter would be incomplete without noting that there is a "Chair of the Board" for my friends and family network. My Chair of the Board is my wife, Teresa Ferrell. If it were not for her numerous unselfish acts, this book and my life as I currently know it wouldn't be possible. My story would have an entirely different slant. I'm grateful and infinitely appreciative of her support, kindness and love, which she extends to me on a daily basis. The road would surely be a much bumpier ride without her as the copilot!

Have you connected with your global village? Do you have a mastermind alliance? Is there a copilot in your present or future plans? If you have answered no to any of these questions, I strongly suggest that you discover ways to make prudent changes to your paradigm.

You gain exponential growth through the help of having the right people in your life. John F. Kennedy had his father, Joseph and his brother Bobby. Tiger Woods had his mother, Kultida and his father, Earl, mentoring him and preparing him for greatness. Mary Lou Retton had the support of her parents and famous gymnastics coach, Bela Karolyi, helping her to catapult into Olympic success.

Who are the people in your camp? You must make this discovery as you continue to navigate through the mine fields of life.

Should you consider making minor to major overhauls to your personal human resources team? Sammy Davis Jr., Dean Martin, Frank Sinatra and Peter Lawford were all superstars in their own right. Nevertheless, they became legendary mega-stars by banding together and taking their team on the road. This group called themselves the "Rat Pack."

One could imagine that they totally bought into the power of the second-family influence and lived their lives in respect of it. They created their own magical village and accepted many others into their group. Sinatra used his powerful connections to break down long-standing barriers for other members in the group. We could liken their devotion to one another to having a super-strength connection of friends and family. How's this for the village shining its light?

I don't believe it is a coincidence that each member of the Rat Pack became a global player in the international community - well before it was fashionable. As you consider expanding your own global community, take out a sharp pencil and write down your second-family influences. Then let the Law of Communication work in your favor. Find the best ways of leaving this group feeling good about you and they will help you to live your dreams.

Key Action Steps
Friends and Family: A Global Community - The Village Shines the Light

Action Step 1
Nurture significant-other influences

Take the time to allow for significant-other influences and create premium-class, second-family options. Your discovery and participation in these families will bring you a lifetime of joy and opportunity!

Action Step 2
Let the village shine the light

As you continue to embrace second-family opportunities, take the time to choose your role models and mentors wisely. Become a great leader through self-improvement and let the wisdom of the village shine its light on your development efforts.

Action Step 3
Adhere to the three P's:
Planning, Passion and Perseverance

Opportunity for the acquisition of high-quality, second-family and global community connections arises from your desire to welcome them. You must proceed with a burning desire in order to receive the gifts from these groups. The best push forward starts with planning, passion and perseverance - the three P's of success!

Action Step 4
Treat everyone with respect:
you are one handshake away from a different lifestyle

You are one handshake away from a different lifestyle. Always treat the people that you meet with respect and appreciation. As you are shaking the hands of friends, colleagues and strangers, you can never be absolutely sure which one of those hands represents the hand up to freedom and fortune. It is also entirely possible that you are the hand that brings freedom and fortune to others. Accepting this theory will help shape how you feel about your future and what you are able to do to steer it in the right direction.

Action Step 5
Shift lives forward through personal branding

Most people enjoy the company of positive-energy personalities. We can all gain strength from the gift of energy that such personalities leave behind. Create an attractive behavior style that lends itself to personal branding and shifts lives forward. Your branded personality can be a source of energy for others.

As you continue to improve upon increasing the quality of your personal branding, you will often leave others feeling good.

Summary Points
Friends and Family: A Global Community -
The Village Shines the Light

1. The key to significant-other influences is found in
   second families

2. Let the three P's work for you: Planning, Passion
   and Perseverance - the village shines the light
   on your success path

3. Choose your villagers prudently: your growth
   and synergy depend on the quality of the village;
   your destiny is either accelerated or thwarted by
   the direction and instruction you receive from
   the village

4. You truly are one handshake away from an entirely
   different lifestyle

5. Elect to shift lives forward through positive personal
   branding

Affirmations
Moments for Reflection

1. I remain open to the discovery of high-quality, second-family influences

2. I willingly step into the light shone by the village

3. I practice the wisdom of the three P's on a daily basis

4. I submit to and offer, the one handshake away from a different life theory

5. I make a conscious effort to develop a personality worthy of branding

Chapter 10

Can You Say Attitude? Your Attitude Can Kill You - Check Your Pulse

Have you ever had someone give you a "full-on facial?" I mean an attitude facial? By this, I mean that they really gave you a face full of attitude. What about the time you entered your local convenience store and the clerk who sells you the beef-jerky and chewing gum continues a long-running conversation with her best friend and coworker, the twenty-something, gum-smacking nightclub queen? All of this without the slightest notion of a simple "hello" or mention of: "Did you find everything that you were looking for?"

The convenience in the term "convenience store" wasn't coined to represent what would be convenient for the clerks or employees. It was conceived, of course, to convey the idea of hassle-free shopping and convenience for the customer. But the scene described has become far too familiar and boils down to the need for a pure attitude adjustment. It is rude to continue a personal conversation with a coworker in the presence of a client - a client who is waiting to be served, no doubt.

I have seen the persistent presence of bad attitudes whether I'm spending two dollars on a loaf of bread or 22 thousand dollars on a new vehicle. I recommend that you take a moment and check your attitude pulse. Checking your pulse is akin to measuring your physical, mental and spiritual barometer. When you check your pulse on a situation, you are seeking to determine how you feel about others or the circumstance in which you find yourself. You discover how it may be affecting you and your environment.

Pulse checking is also about taking the time to ensure that you aren't in need of an attitude adjustment. Could something in your character or actions be inviting the chance of opening the floodgates of negative energy? An honest pulse check may be just what the doctor ordered to clear the air. This is a simple method of searching within for a sense of balance. It might save you from embarrassment or wrongful actions on your part. Unless you have resigned yourself to living a totally miserable life, no one wants to wade in the waters of bad attitudes or bad-energy types.

Oftentimes, we encounter skirmishes in relationships that are loaded with arrogance. Arrogant people are full of self-importance and you rarely get them to empathize with others. They simply cannot see past themselves. The world rotates best, when it rotates solely around them! I have found that the most effective way to deal with arrogant types is to let them have the limelight, largely because they wouldn't dare share it anyway. Limit exposure, especially one-on-one exposure, to arrogant personality types. This will help relieve the pain of their company. Laying arrogance on others is not a good way to leave people feeling!

Enduring a bad attitude or arrogant personality is like being subjected to a bad smell. Quite frankly, IT STINKS and nobody likes it! Nobody wins when bad attitudes are allowed to poison the environment. People with attitude issues suffer because they make themselves miserable by internalizing their rotten dispositions. If you allow the negative energy exchange, they will make you ill with this easily transmittable virus that I call "negative-itis."

Don't allow others to take their toxic attitudes and poison your environment. It will sap your energy quicker than the blink of an eye. Oftentimes, our moods are a consequence of continued exposure to those with dark energy. We may not realize that their negative-itis has crept into our world and taken over our mental programming.

This is when you find someone else's programming on your personal TV station. How silly is this? Silly as it may be, this happens so quickly and easily that most folks don't notice until the virus has been allowed to contaminate their spirits and permeate their souls. But eventually you realize that you are feeling bad, even though, until you trace the origin, you don't know why you feel this way. Take note of attitudinal changes as you move through time and space and take whatever measures might be necessary for correction. Whenever an energy thief who is steeped in the virus of negative-itis attempts a mind-infecting ploy, protect yourself.

The antidote is rarely a simple task of avoiding the energy thieves. Consequently, sometimes a fair amount of ingesting the toxins emitted by those in need of an attitude adjustment is unavoidable. However, there is a way to minimize your contact with them.

The key is to sniff out trouble early and find the best way to reduce the exposure to the people, the situation - or, oftentimes, both! Dispel the toxic fumes of bad behavior. A quick determination of the fundamental differences between you and others of this toxic ilk will help you launch your exit strategy. The keys to a graceful exit are your best words deployed with care.

In other words, be tactful as you navigate through - and out of - this situation. This is not the time to return fire with fire. "Tact is the knack of making a point without making an enemy." This comment from Sir Isaac Newton is well taken. Your tactful reply and exit strategy will remove you from the negative virus and leave a little something positive behind for the infected person to chew on. You will leave them feeling better, if not good! But leave them nevertheless...

"Tact is the knack of making a point without making an ememy."

- Sir Isaac Newton

What emotions come into play whenever you are served up a fresh, hot plate of bad attitude? Might you be feeling, perhaps, anger, frustration, anxiety, anguish, disdain, or fear? None of these aforementioned emotions are nice to be left with. Oftentimes, a simple checking of your pulse, attitude adjustment, a time-out, or a couple of good deep breaths can save you a lifetime of heartache from the results of your own attitude and reactions.

Never let toxic energy thieves take up residency in your mental neighborhood. This is truly the family that you don't want living on your block. Once they move in, all the good neighbors flee and move to higher ground - where the air is much cleaner! Checking your pulse, surveying the tone of the environment and refusing to accept toxicity are strong defenses for guarding the mental peace and healthy environment we all crave.

As you go through life, it is unavoidable that you will run across people whom you aren't comfortable with. To put it bluntly, you just don't like them and it may not have anything to do with what they have done or said to you. Conversely, the shoe could easily fit on the other foot. There will be people who you meet who plainly don't like you either! The 100-thousand-dollar question is, "What can you do about this observable fact?"

The first step is to discover common ground. Always endeavor to build your relationship on something you can agree upon. Most people enjoy the company of others they feel they can relate to. In the most challenging of circumstances there are always some overlapping areas of interest. Even if infinitesimal, these are areas in which you may be able to establish a bond with those who rub you the wrong way.

You are not looking to turn the relationship into "bosom buddies." Your definitive goal is to hammer out an amicable connection that serves the greater good. Following these initial steps in relationship building with difficult people will help you forge a rapport with those you do not like.

This suggestion is not intended to indicate that you will get along well with everyone. Rather, its major premise is to ensure you don't subvert yourself as you strive to live your best life now! As you form associations with the various people you meet during your travels, you can never be too sure of how you may be able to help one another, in spite of your personality differences. Thinking otherwise is foolish and truly could work against you. Your opportunity for receiving help from those you shut out at first glance is quite likely lost forever!

You always have to leave people, even the difficult ones, with an "out." In a similar vein, Frederick C. Elliott, Founder and Chairman of the EMI Group, shared a wonderful quote by the famous Indian Chief, Sitting Bull: "To leave a man with his dignity is above all things." These ways of treating others, together with the one handshake away theory I profiled in Chapter 9, might represent the tipping point in your personal and professional endeavors.

"To leave a man with his dignity is above all things

Sitting Bull

Your attitude can kill you

I recently read an extremely tragic story in the newspaper about a case of bad attitude resulting in the killing of one man and the imprisonment of another. As the story goes, an elderly man was attempting to pull into a gas station and car wash for service. A young woman driving a fancy car with her two kids in it inadvertently cut him off. The man began shouting nasty epithets at the young woman. His attitude was moving toward full rage as he was determined to show her how she had wronged him by getting into the space ahead of him. The woman became scared and began to panic. She didn't know how far the man's rage would escalate.

In short order, she whipped out her cell phone and called her husband, an up-and-coming entrepreneur. The husband dropped everything at work and rushed to the aid of his wife and children.

Upon his arrival, attitudes began to flair out of control, which culminated in the younger man pushing the elder one. The latter fell to the ground, bumped his head and died as a result of the fall. The young professional ended up in jail with no way to run his business and support his family. And all of this happened because the people involved never took a fraction of a second to check their pulses. They failed to ask themselves, "Is there another way to escape from this toxic environment or to remove the hostile venomous communication?"

The elderly man was killed because he allowed his attitude to make a young husband and wife feel threatened by his behavior. The couple's responses also resulted in a tragic end. The young couple was left to deal with a prison sentence for the husband, whose his life as he knew it was ended the moment that he put his hands on the elderly man in a hostile fashion. The whole situation spiraled out of control as a result of attitudes not remaining in check.

I share this story with you in order to place a special emphasis on checking your attitudinal pulse. I invite you to explore taking corrective measures either to neutralize negative energy and atmosphere or to take the quickest escape route. I'm sure the young professional has replayed that situation hundreds of times in his mind and has found just as many alternate scenarios that would have maintained his freedom. Attitude is a choice. There are a number of embedded messages in this story. Please examine below a sampling of messages, which I call JessTalk "keepers":

JessTalk keepers will help you develop and nurture the best attitude

1. Understand how you are feeling when someone is negatively affecting your environment

2. Always ask yourself: "How can I neutralize a situation with someone who has a bad attitude and who has poisoned the environment?"

3. Explore this: Has your open-door policy left you open to receiving everyone else's negative releasing?

4. Be very careful about those you surround yourself with. Others can both lift you up and bring you crashing down

5. Remain optimistic, even during the worst of times; everything eventually passes

6. If you are saddled with a loss, keep only the lesson and move on

7. Take in the most positive nurturing to preserve your attitude: eating right, exercising, quality reading, proper rest and choosing the best environments for your optimum life balance

8. Remember: Positive thinking leads to positive doing

Checking your pulse

Checking your pulse is so important for influencing the best way to leave yourself and others feeling that it deserves its own section in this book. Checking your pulse is an integral part of the concept of how you leave them feeling. Checking your pulse leads to accepting truth and backing it up with responsible action, which paves the way to living a life of leaving others feeling good.

Whenever you exercise the gift of leaving others feeling good, they in turn will be inclined to leave you feeling good. The win/win concept must have roots in this philosophy. You can't change others. But with concerted effort, backed with conviction, emotion and, last but certainly not least, passion, you will systematically improve the quality of your own life. Your light will shine bright enough to warm the hearts of others, while leaving you ample to live on!

Checking your pulse may be one of the best interpersonal skills you can learn. In order to become a healthy contributor to relationships and to attain situational management, checking yourself and measuring your reactions lead on to ultimate success.

Checking your pulse includes asking yourself some simple, but often overlooked, questions: "How do I feel today? Where do I stand with myself? What talents and gifts am I going to offer myself and the world today? Will I be poised to have a good day no matter what? Or will I let the day dictate to me what it intends to bring me? Will I allow self-doubt to find a home within me and distort reality?" (This of course would place you in a position of extreme weakness, as your actions fail to match the reality of any situation in which you become involved.)

Don't let self-delusion convince you that you are okay when you aren't. On the other hand, don't let self-doubt tell you that you aren't worthy. When is it best to check your ego at the door? Would you check your level of ego with your spouse, boss or business partner? What type of paradigm could you create for yourself and others if you maintained a respectably balanced ego?

As you might have come to notice, there are many

questions that one must explore to serve the notion of checking your pulse. Checking your pulse is about asking the tough questions and managing the solutions to which they point. This section of the book is not about giving you "turn-key" answers. It is intended to help you internalize the right questions and answer them. Customizing your solutions in life will serve you well, as you personally determine the best way to leave yourself and others feeling good.

What is your system for overcoming challenges? Do you operate from the standpoint of measuring your situation carefully before deciding on a course of action? In other words, do you learn to read people and situations by using your human measuring stick, your internal barometer? Focus on clues other than verbal communication from others to determine where you stand with people. Follow your intuition when turning on your "read meter," or checking your pulse. There is a direct and clear answer to life's challenges that is situated between your intuition and the right solution.

What is your code? Create a set of virtues that allow you to become the type of person that others feel comfortable befriending. Continue to raise the bar on your expectations of yourself as you include your virtues in your life plan. As I work with my JessTalk clients, I help them develop or shape a set of virtues that lead to achieving the life they deserve. The following represent the JessTalk virtues:

The "HAVIT" code

Humility: I remain appreciative and humble when connecting with other people

Attitude: I treat others the way they want to be treated - and they tell me

Value: Competent core values drive my endeavors and I expect excellence

Integrity: I commit to do what I say I will do

Time: I respect this precious commodity and share it in my quality relationships

I have continued to hone my HAVIT Code over the past forty years and I have discovered that the more I learn, the more there is to know. Although I have built a solid foundation, in my efforts to improve my personal and professional stock, I'm constantly discovering subtle nuances of life. Some people set goals and just as they are reaching their goals, they let up. This may be a sign of human nature. However, you can't afford to let up on your goals; they ultimately define your person.

Key Action Steps
Can You Say Attitude? Your Attitude Can Kill You - Check Your Pulse

Action Step 1
Maintain an excellent attitude - attitude determines altitude

The height of your ceiling of opportunities is determined by the attitude you possess. Strive to develop and maintain a fresh and positive attitude, especially when you are with others. Make sure you are aware of the changing landscape of your social environments and make the proper adjustments in order to modulate your attitude as needed.

Action Step 2
Check your pulse often

As mentioned before, we all run across difficult personality types. The concept of checking your pulse offers you the ability to ensure that you have not become like one of the difficult personalities you encounter. Take precautionary measures to ensure that nothing in your character invites negative-energy types. Remember to check your pulse often.

Action Step 3
Run your own personal program

We tend to take on some of the characteristics of those we surround ourselves with. Be careful to surround yourself with people whom you admire. Also admire them for the type of personal programs they run on. Choose people who stand for integrity, sincerity, warmth and other attractive human qualities. Design your character to fit the desires of your own personal programming. Never run another person's negative program on your life's TV station.

Action Step 4
Protect your mental attitude from toxic energy thieves

There will always be that fraction of the human race that tends to drain the life from your soul. They are what I call toxic energy thieves. Keep your time with these people brief and don't allow them to steal away your energy. Maintain a good exit strategy for those unavoidable times when you may encounter a toxic energy thief.

Action Step 5
Develop your life code and virtues

I have discovered that those people who have not developed a life code often find themselves in trouble. Having no code can be a dark and lonely place to live. Develop a code for how you do things. Decide for yourself what works for you and what you refuse to accept. Back this code up with a set of virtues that help keep you on target for living your best life code.

Summary Points
Can You Say Attitude? Your Attitude Can Kill You
- Check Your Pulse

1. Your attitude will determine your altitude;
   how high will you rise?

2. Checking yourself or checking your attitudinal
   pulse, aids your attitude adjustment

3. Don't let the bad attitudes of others determine the
   programming of your personal TV station

4. Protect your mental attitude by refusing to associate
   with toxic energy thieves

5. Develop a code for living the life you desire;
   establish virtues for support

Affirmations
Moments for Reflection

1. I am sharing my positive attitude with others while
   increasing my altitude

2. I keep a close watch on my attitude

3. I run my own personal program

4. I choose to stay away from toxic energy thieves

5. My life code and virtues evolve daily

Chapter 11

The Sixth Essential Law of Life
The Law of Cause and Effect

The sixth essential law of life, the Law of Cause and Effect is one of the laws that allow you to sit in the driver's seat of life. When you place both hands on the wheel and put the pedal to the metal, your best life happens now!

The choices you make with respect to this law will determine the quality of life you live. We briefly touched upon this law in the introduction to this book. Although all the other laws play equally important roles in the evolution of your life, the Law of Cause and Effect truly and continually offers you the opportunity to create the life you desire via the process of sowing and reaping.

The Law of Cause and Effect is also known as karma. Karma is a concept in several eastern religions that comprises the entire cycle of cause and effect. Karma literally means "deed" or "act," and it more broadly covers the universal Law of Cause and Effect. Think of it this way, karma is the sum of all that an individual has done and all that he or she is currently doing. The effect of those deeds actively creates present and future experiences.

Much like the other laws noted in this book, karma works even if you are not aware of it. What are you doing right now to create the life and destiny you desire? You are responsible; avoid blaming others who you feel may have contributed to your poor quality of life. Take responsibility for your own fate.

For example, I chose to use the power of the village to propel me forward in life. It was my choice to seek help and embrace that choice along with the wisdom of the village. While I have been helped exponentially as a result of my choices, the true power lies in my willingness to choose those options.

I am responsible for my own life! I continually challenge myself to live the life I desire. I choose to use the principles and power of the how you leave them feeling concept to move me along the success journey at a pace that disallows slowing down. Again, this is my choice and I am responsible. We are each responsible for our own karma.

The Law of Cause and Effect, or karma, has strong religious roots. The idea of karma is central to India in the following religions: Hinduism, Sikhism, Buddhism and Jainism. While the Law of Cause and Effect is firmly entrenched in the Eastern religions, it has found deep roots in Western culture as well. Millions of people have adopted the karma theory or the Law of Cause and Effect as part of their psyches. Oftentimes, people with no religious background adopt these laws. The Law of Cause and Effect and spirituality are often spoken of in the same context.

The Law of Cause and Effect says that everything happens for a reason. For every effect in your life, there is a cause, or clearly identifiable basis. As you consider the success journey, take heed of the Law of Cause and Effect. This law helps you to discover the keys to success through education, as well as through exposure to and modeling of, successful people. Simply by replicating their acts, you, too, can create the same success paradigm.

Once you have clearly defined your major purpose in life, backed with plans of action, it is just a matter of time and maturity before you are living the life of your design. Planting the seeds of fate is an investment in living your best life - and it starts with your choices. The people you choose to connect with and the places you go will dramatically help shape the quality of your world.

A few years ago I decided to trade in the mythical security of the corporate world for a life of freedom and entrepreneurship. I closely examined the people I was surrounded by and the environments that I spent the "lion's share" of my time in. Upon examination I made some difficult choices. I took the time to create a Lifestyle Conversion and Transition Dossier to help this process of change. The process is profiled as follows:

Fundamental questions in order to determine your right path

1. Where am I now?

2. Where would I like to be?

3. How am I going to get there?

This Lifestyle Conversion and Transition Dossier is a seventy-five page report and is intended to answer the questions above. The following headings represent the content of this dossier:

Lifestyle Conversion and Transition Dossier

1. Lifestyle Conversion and Transition Thesis

2. Lifetime Plan For Ensuring Financial Security

3. Mastermind Alliance (Friends and Family, Second-Family Influences)

4. Goals and Objectives - Targets and Confirmation Dates

5. Discovery and Action Plan Link - Discovering the Leaders in My New Field

6. Thinking-Outside-the-Box Model (Stretching the Vision)

7. Motivational Stories Bank

8. Mantras, Themes and Topics

9. Relationship Marketing Contacts

10. Book Bank: Educational Materials to Increase Knowledge in My Field

11. Industry Leaders Outreach Correspondence

12. Planned Speaking Engagements

13. Cash Flow Statements

14. Net Worth Statement

15. Fico Scores

I isolated each of the above areas and then put them together to be used as a road map in order to merge onto the success superhighway. If you are looking to make profound changes in your life, do not consider it without a comprehensive plan.

There are too many twists and turns on the turnpike of life to travel without the protection of proper planning. Each of the points listed in the Lifestyle Conversion and Transition Dossier must be examined in detail and brought to full maturity in order to benefit from the respective categories. Assembling the carefully selected components brings unmatched synergy to your collective thoughts and serves as the best road map toward effective change and clarity on the success journey.

I had a clear understanding that my mission was to create a professional speaking company - one whose

sole aim was to help others bring clarity, focus and purpose to their lives. My road map was set and the next
task was full exposure to the best minds in my new
field.

After careful study of the best professional speakers and
motivators in the world, my karma brought me to the
work of Brian Tracy. Tracy is one of the most brilliant
and captivating professional speakers and authors of our
time.

I met Tracy at a leadership conference a couple of sum-
mers ago. We shared a powerful conversation, which
launched yet another defining moment for me. The
quest to help as many people as possible by using effective listening skills and the power of words is a true
manifestation of my best work to date.

Tracy forcefully encouraged me to continue on my path.
It was a special certification from one of the industry's
giants. That conversation is replicated as follows:

Jesse
Hello, Mr. Tracy, my name is Jesse Ferrell. It is a real
pleasure to meet you.

Brian
Hello, Jesse, please call me Brian.

Jesse
Brian, I must tell you: You have done more for me in
one audio listening program from your book "Action
Strategies for Personal Achievement" than I received
in multiple college degrees.

Brian
Really? Tell me more.

Jesse
I began to change my thinking regarding what I could

do to take control of my life within the first fifteen minutes of your book. By the time I finished the first cassette, I had launched a new directive and set lofty, yet achievable, goals.

Brian
Wow! That is fascinating. I'm glad that I could help you.

Jesse
Help? You did much more than help. By the time I finished the full audio program, I emerged on the other side of the reading with an entirely different lifestyle and a new life plan.

Brian
So tell me, Jesse, what do you do for a living now?

Jesse
I launched a professional speaking company in order to help others, in the same vein that you have helped me! Along with a life-coaching program, I schedule domestic and international speaking engagements for companies and individuals in our emerging world of global commerce. I think of myself as a global thinker.

Brian
Do you ever use any of my stuff on the road?

Jesse
Yes, in fact I do! And I always remember to credit you as the source of the information used.

Brian
Well, the next time you are on the road and you use any of my material, you tell the audience that your friend Brian said it was okay for you to use anything that I create!

Jesse

Thanks, Brian, that is an awesome honor. I will take you up on your offer!

Brian

Do you have a business card on hand?

Jesse

If you will give me a moment, I can retrieve my business cards. Here are five different business cards, representing five distinct business ventures that I'm involved in. Together they represent what I call my "Quantum Strength Pillars." (The following represents the business cards that I handed Tracy.)

1. President, JessTalk Speaking Services LLC,
   - Las Vegas, Nevada

2. EMI Group - International Advisor and Performance Coach - Orangeville, Canada and the Dominican Republic

3. Ann Lee & Associates Alliance Partner
   - Sr. National Advisor & Performance Coach, Houston, Texas

4. University of Nevada, Adjunct Professor
   - Las Vegas, Nevada

5. Harrah's Entertainment Inc. - Independent Casino Marketing Representative, Las Vegas, Nevada

Brian

Impressive!

Jesse

You started all of this, after motivating and inspiring me. You stirred up my entrepreneurial juices! And I believed in your concepts. Thank you.

Brian
You will hear from me.

Jesse
I will count on it!

This conversation I had with Tracy was magical! Here I was standing toe-to-toe with my latest and strongest role model and, by the grace of my faith and respect for the universal Laws of Cause and Effect, my karma was yet again reinventing my potential.

Tracy willingly and graciously signed on as a member of my global village. The community is enriched by his inclusion. He was quite comfortable with ushering in a fresh and vibrant second-family relationship. Here was the Cause and Effect Theory in action! All the count-less hours of reading a smorgasbord of powerful authors, with Tracy leading the pack, represented the Cause. Tracy's willingness to lend a hand, where and when he could, was the Effect. The karma theory works, even when you are still learning the essential laws of life.

Following this magical conversation, Tracy sent me his book, Change Your Thinking, Change Your Life, in appreciation of our powerful conversation. His book, which I warmly received, came with the following cor-respondence:

Handwritten note on stationary:
From the desk of Brian Tracy

Jesse,
It was a real pleasure meeting you.
You are a great inspiration. Keep up the great work.

Kind Regards,

Brian

Handwritten note on the first page of Tracy's book -
"Change Your Thinking, Change Your Life"

August 4, 2004

Jesse,
Congratulations on your success! I wish you all the
best of health, happiness and prosperity in the exciting
years ahead.
Hang in There!

Brian Tracy

Wow! Tracy pushed me to yet another pivotal moment
with this extraordinary gift of kindness. I was overwhelmed with joy. You might imagine that I was lev-
itating with inspiration, as Tracy's outreach solidified
my belief in the strong principles we both accepted
as truth. The seven essential laws of life were being
manifested and I was keenly aware of this. My understanding of how to live in the here and now made the
precious minutes after unwrapping Tracy's gift a defining moment! I will never forget it. As I have said earlier
in this book, "People may not always remember what
you have done, but they will always remember how you
made them feel!"

This opened the door for additional correspondence
with Tracy and through each communication, I continue to grow stronger in leaps and bounds. I fully
submit to this sixth essential law of life, the Law of
Cause and Effect. I enjoy the building process. I like
moving the colors around on the canvas of life in
order to reap the effects of a life that has been custom-
designed!

I took the liberty of attending another leadership conference sponsored by Tracy approximately a year after
meeting him at my first leadership conference. I was

again given the opportunity to speak with him during break time at his professional speaking engagement.

This dialogue offered a different slant from our first conversation. We spoke about various time-management tools that interested us both. We shared our ideas on creating systems that foster growth in ourselves and in the people we encounter in our life-coaching programs. This conversation ended with Tracy asking me to send him my JessTalk Lifestyle Portfolio, which I designed to help the clients on the JessTalk Coaching Lifestyles Program.

Not long after this conversation, I received another gift from Tracy. He sent me his book, Many Miles To Go. In his classic and genuine style, Tracy included a follow-up observation and critique of the JessTalk Lifestyle Portfolio and a personal handwritten note.

In honor and respect for Tracy, I want to share the power of his communication. I also share Tracy's notes with you in order to inspire you to learn from his amazing gifts of communication and to encourage you to start building your own second-family influences now!

Note on Brian Tracy international stationary:

June 16, 2005

Jesse,
Thank you very much for sending me your amazing "Quantum Strength Pillars & Flow Chart." It is the most complete and comprehensive approach to personal, business and life management that I have ever seen.

The only danger of such a plan is that it can become overwhelming. In my coaching programs, I train people to focus on simplicity. We teach the "Law of Three," *which says that there are only three major things you do in any area that account for 90% or more of the results.*

Your job is to determine the three most important things and then to focus single-mindedly on them, continually improving your performance in each area.

Jess, I wish you the very best of continued success in everything you do. You are definitely on the right track. Keep up the great work!

Kind regards,
Brian Tracy

Handwritten note on the first page of Tracy's book - "Many Miles To Go":

June 15, 2005

Jesse,
Congratulations! You are a remarkable man. I wish you every success on your own personal journey.

Best regards,
Brian Tracy

When I received the first book and positive endorsement from Tracy, as I mentioned, I was overwhelmed. But to have him duplicate his gift in an entirely different situation left me with chills of excitement. Above all other examples cited here in my own book, How You Leave Them Feeling, Tracy's actions left me feeling fantastic. The many positive reminders of the gift of how Tracy has left me feeling are permanently etched into my soul. He has sincerely put into motion the Law of Cause and Effect and I'm a proud benefactor of his kindness and wisdom. I will continue to read materials produced by Tracy; he is a true "Renaissance man" and I treasure his leadership!

Who are your chosen archetypes? Who will help you make the crossover onto the superhighway of life? How will you connect with them? As you seek to discover these answers, think about this sixth essential law of life, the Law of Cause and Effect. Make it count when, where and how you need it!

Key Action Steps
The Law of Cause and Effect

Action Step 1
Take responsibility: the Law of Cause and Effect gives you the key

The Law of Cause and Effect gives you the key to life by placing you squarely in the driver's seat. Take responsibility for your own life now. Plant the seeds today of how you want to live in the future. Remember to rejoice in the moment as you continually prepare for a bright future. Let the karma theory - the Law of Cause and Effect - serve you well.

Action Step 2
Make good choices

Allow your best choices to set the standard for the type of life you want to live. With respect to the karma theory, expend the necessary energy researching and thinking about the information that will lead you to the life you desire. At the end of the day, it is the quality of your choices that make the difference in life.

Action Step 3
Know that karma and the Law of Cause and Effect are the same

The karma theory and the Law of Cause and Effect are

governed by the same principles. Take the time to build your full understanding of these universal principles. The quality of your current and future life depends on your understanding of these laws.

Action Step 4
Determine where you are

As you look to build a quality future, start your quest by fully understanding where you are in life. Take an assessment of where you stand in the most critical areas of your life. Build your development plan from the basis of knowing your true starting point. A reality check and a solid determination of where you are will put you on a steady success journey.

Action Step 5
Develop your lifestyle plan

If you are looking to make major changes in your life, you will need the aid of a Lifestyle Conversion and Transition Dossier. This is your initial lifestyle plan that helps you move from where you are to where you desire to be. Take the time to create a comprehensive plan. Use the theory of backwards planning in order to ensure that you don't miss steps along the way.

Summary Points
The Sixth Essential Law of Life
The Law of Cause and Effect

1. The Law of Cause and Effect allows you to sit in the driver's seat of life

2. The choices you make in relation to the Law of Cause and Effect will have a large impact on the quality of your life

3. The karma theory and the Law of Cause and Effect are essentially the same

4. Determine where you are before you figure out where you are going

5. You will see your best goals attained via the development of a lifestyle plan

Affirmations
Moments for Reflection

1. I have respect for and live by, the principles of the karma theory

2. I make prudent choices to support the life I desire

3. I use the Law of Cause and Effect to usher in an attractive lifestyle

4. I know exactly where I am on the success journey at all times

5. My lifestyle plan is vibrant and brings consistent positive results

Chapter 12

Develop a Passion for Leaving Everything - and Everyone - Better Than You Found Them

I discovered this life objective nearly forty years ago. You must make a very strong commitment to read situations and people well in order to have any success with this goal. Your power of intention must be unwavering. While none of us behave in a perfect fashion 100 percent of the time, this is no excuse for not honoring the goal of leaving both situations and people better than you found them.

Quite contrary to attempting to be perfect, the rule of leaving everything and everyone better than you found them, speaks to the power of your thought. Even just the idea of moving through life as a representative of constant improvement sets you apart. Your intent alone distinguishes you from those who merely follow the herd.

Most people never create any virtues for living their lives. The fact that you are reading this book already puts you in the "short line" of those headed directly for success. Your karma has brought you to this source in order to discover more truths. Your thinking is already in alignment with success, or it is heading in the right direction - like the speed of light!

The goal of leaving everyone and everything better than you found them says more about what you think of yourself and how you choose to govern your life, than what it does for the benefactors of your actions. To put it plainly, although others will benefit from your goals and actions, you will feel a gratifying calm as you continue to push the objective of leaving things and people better than you found them.

Have you heard the saying, "Practice makes perfect?"

Are you ready for a twist to that statement? How about, "Perfect practice, makes practice perfect!" Map out your intentions before stumbling through life and finding yourself somewhere you don't intend to be. Identify the right type of ideals and virtues, then go to work on creating them in yourself and others.

What kind of world would we live in if more people undertook this quest for their virtues? How much better off would we all be? This is the perfect place to reiterate the question, "What kind of world would this be if everyone in it were just like me?" Imagine a world in which the majority of the population embarked on a campaign of leaving everything and everyone better than they found them.

How much trash would you see others step over? How many wars would be avoided and decided against in excellent communication forums? How many families would move from the "norm of dysfunction" to the rarity of beauty and nurturing? Could you imagine the effects on the environment and human nature? There would be cleaner rivers, oceans, mountains and parks. There would be happier people.

I realize it would be naive to assume that swift and all-encompassing improvement is truly possible. But what if we started by making subtle changes that could lead to a big difference? What if only those who read this book and those they shared it with assumed the objective of leaving things and people better than they found them? At the very least, this movement would positively change the nature of our immediate surroundings.

Think about it: Your relationships would improve dramatically, your home life would strengthen and your work and play environments would be enhanced as well. How you feel about yourself would take a boost as a result of this trickle-down effect.

The aim of leaving everything and everyone better than you found them will do more to change how you navigate through the mine fields of life than most other ideals you might consider. Once you have determined where to begin, waste not a minute. Launch your awareness campaign of betterment and watch your lifestyle meter rise!

As I noted earlier, I have been making every effort to leave everything and everyone better than I found them for more than forty years. With that said, I have literally hundreds of stories that I could share with you regarding the results of these efforts. The story, however, that most stands out in my "life vault" is that of Allan Ludwig. This story exemplifies my belief in the value of how you leave them feeling!

Allan grew up in the same small town in northern Nevada - in Hawthorne - as I did. He was born into a family of three sisters. While all of his sisters were born without any complications, he was not so fortunate. He was diagnosed with a developmental disability that affects him mentally. He also suffers from seizures as a result of epilepsy. The seizures are grand mal, petty mal and petite; they can flare up at any time and are most often followed by a quick trip to the emergency room for recovery.

Most folks in Hawthorne considered Allan to be quite different from other people. I refused to label this young man and decided to treat him just as I would any other member of his family. I spent most of my childhood days in Hawthorne painting and drawing. I always looked for coaching and guidance to improve my artistic abilities. As mentioned earlier, I found that tutelage in Mrs. Ludwig Peterson, Allan's mother. She was very accommodating with her time and patience. I was afforded the luxury of making the long journey to her home about three to four times per week. She was always ready to critique my latest creation. These trips became more frequent during my senior year of high school, as I was preparing for university scholarships.

As a young boy, Allan was always waiting outside to see me off with a joke or two. Although he was just twelve, I always devoted the time required to allow him to fully communicate with me. He had a schoolboy charm and his looks and demeanor reminded me of Opie Taylor of the Andy Griffith Show. Even when his jokes were not very funny, I was amused that he would even make the effort.

My goal was to always leave him in better spirits than I found him, mostly through the act of listening. After leaving Hawthorne at 17 and heading for the University of Nevada, Las Vegas, I lost touch with Allan, even though I maintained contact with Mrs. Ludwig Peterson.

In June of 2004, I went to my mailbox and discovered a letter from, of all people, Allan Ludwig. For the life of me, I could not figure out why, after having no communication for the past twenty-seven years, he would be reaching out to me. Rather than my telling you a long story, read his letter, which follows:

First Page of Allan's Letter

DeaR JeSS,E
HI. How ARe you doing? IT.S

Allan. how is youR JoB Going
I HoPe Good. I Have SomeThing
FoR you BuT you will get IT
when you Read This LeTTeR
HA-HA.

I would Like You To Be

MY BesT Man aT MY

Wedding pleas I
SuRe would LIke

That Allan Ludwig

Phon (307) 433-0494

canI geT youR

PHONe #NuMBeR.

(OVER)

Back Page of Allan's Letter

The Wedding is
August 14Th 2004

Pleas Call Need To Talk
To you, do you have a Blue
Suit ThaTs The coloR of mine

Okay Thank you

Allan & ChRisTy

Photo Included in Letter

Back of Photo

Alan & christy
wont four ½ years befor
geting hitched together.

Lessie Bestman

8-14-04

I was astonished to learn that Allan wanted me to be the best man at his wedding. I was very excited to call him to find out how he came to choose me to play such an awesome role at a very important time in his life.

I made the call within minutes of receiving the letter. His fiancée, Christy, answered the phone. As I made my introduction to her, she blurted out, "Allan has told everyone in Cheyenne, Wyoming, that you are his best friend in the whole wide world."

I was surprised to hear this revelation since I had not spoken to Allan for such a long time. As I was transitioning into a young man on my way to college, he was still a little boy who had a plethora of medical issues. We were not given the luxury of being close to one another in age or of growing up in the same social circles. But he somehow remembered our short talks and the respect that I always paid him. He carried that respect with him everywhere he went.

After a lengthy conversation with Christy, she passed the phone to Ludwig. I said to him, "Before I say yes to this thing, you just have to tell me, what in the world made you choose me as your best man after all this time?"

He didn't hesitate for a fraction of a second and retorted: "Oh…You are sooooo cool!"

Well, needless to say, all those times at the home of my eighth-grade art teacher and the short visits with Allan, had made a difference in both of our worlds. He cherished the respect he had been given and carried it with him everywhere he went. I was blessed with the understanding that the theory of leaving him better than I had found him had hit its target. The twenty-seven years since I had last spoken to Allan were bridged in a ten-minute conversation.

This story is evidence of the power of leaving people better than you found them. And I will always treasure how Allan left me feeling after I learned how much of a difference he felt I made in his life. What will you do in your world in order to make an impact on the lives of others?

Key Action Steps
Develop a Passion for Leaving Everything - and Everyone - Better Than You Found Them

Action Step 1
Leave things and people better than you found them

When you take on the responsibility of leaving everything and everyone better than you found them, you truly honor the word "responsible." By this I mean that you hold yourself accountable for being "able-to-respond" to the notion of improvement. Your actions follow your words and all the things in which you get involved in improve because of your commitment.

Action Step 2
Make the difference with your code

You can make a huge contribution to yourself, your relationships and the world when you take on the discipline of polishing up your code. A positive code governs your actions and helps you stay several steps ahead of trouble. The entire world would be improved by a code that kept us all steps ahead of impending doom as a result of our actions.

Action Step 3
Allow your code to displace dysfunction

Many of the dysfunctional situations I have encountered are a matter of lack of code. Learn to function from a solid base of core values. Eliminate dysfunctional situations by living your code rather than simply being all talk.

Action Step 4
Leave a lasting impression

Take every opportunity to practice the art of leaving situations and people better than you found them. You will leave a lasting impression on others and undoubtedly alter many lives. The story of Allan Ludwig serves as a prime example of this point.

Action Step 5
Give regardless of residual rewards

As you continue endeavoring to leave things and people better than you found them, focus on the responsibility, rather than rewards. The residual rewards will automatically become a part of the scenario of the gift of giving.

Summary Points
Develop a Passion for Leaving Everything - and Everyone - Better Than You Found Them

1. As part of your life code, develop a passion for leaving everything and everyone better than you found them; allow your virtues to stem from this code

2. Ask: "How could my new code and corresponding virtues improve the world?"

3. Dysfunction turns into a classic vantage point when shaped by your code

4. Remember the story of Allan Ludwig when pursuing your passion for leaving situations and people better than you found them; you will make a deep impression

5. The power of leaving everything and everyone better than you found them brings with it a lifetime of residual rewards

Affirmations
Moments for Reflection

1. My commitment to improvement in all areas leaves me feeling good

2. I spend considerable time thinking about and polishing up, my code

3. I live my personal code

4. I enjoy leaving a positive impression on others

5. I value my life code and appreciate the residual rewards that manifest

Chapter 13

The Seventh Essential Law of Life
The Law of Balance

The seventh essential law of life, the Law of Balance, is our final truth in discovering the importance of leaving others feeling good. There is nothing more powerful than knowing you have full control over your life and destiny. When you have created the ability to exercise multiple options for creating the dynamic lifestyle you choose, the gravity of life gets a lot lighter!

Leaving others feeling good cannot manifest fully unless you are operating with maximum efficiency from the source - yourself. Your greatest power for motivating and inspiring others is ignited by jump-starting yourself first! This strategy ensures that you are operating from a strong perspective and solid foundation when you embark upon a campaign of continually feeling good.

When you feel good, your energy is vastly different. It resonates at higher levels and your positive presence is announced long before you enter a room. Remember, "Like attracts like." When you maintain a high-resonating state of being, you attract an abundance of other positive-minded people and life-altering circumstances into your world. The manner in which you take care of yourself is a key component in furthering the process of acquiring balance.

Balance can be viewed in a number of ways. I will start with the concept of simply living a balanced lifestyle. Are you living a balanced lifestyle right now? If you are not living a balanced lifestyle, the next question is: "Why not?" Don't you do everything better when you have an innate sense of self and possess a stronger feeling of balance? Have you ever heard the expression: "A sound body, mind and soul?" This connects right to the principles of living a balanced lifestyle. Simply said, it is much healthier to live a life of abundance versus a life of scarcity. Your attitude and disposition are invigorated by a quality of life supported by the Law of Balance.

The key to living a balanced life is to understand the full paradigm of balance. Although balance is a simple concept to understand, few take the time to learn and benefit from the entire process that is involved.

The keys to living a life of balance can be found in the quest for becoming "bioenvironmentally balanced." Bioenvironmental balancing comprises the coordination of the laws of mental, physical, spiritual and environmental-emotional balancing with the laws of life. This all-encompassing state is elaborated below in the Four Absolute Codes for Living a Bioenvironmentally Balanced Lifestyle and the JessTalk Life Quadrant Model:

The Four Absolute Codes for Living a Bioenvironmentally Balanced Lifestyle
The JessTalk Life Quadrant Model

1. Mental Balancing - this quality of mind strengthens your creativity and stimulates your intellect

2. Physical Balancing - the gift of resilience invigorates all life processes

3. Spiritual Balancing - this, the grounding force, connects self with nature's strengths

4. Environmental-Emotional Balancing - this entails managing your inner feelings and emotional state of being in a world of shifting environments

Bioenvironmentally Balanced Lifestyle

Each of the Four Absolute Codes must be present in varying degrees, respective to your life circumstances and the connection you feel to your right path. Adherence to the kind of balance embodied in each principle creates the best awareness of where you stand in your overall quest for balance!

Living a life of balanced awareness is the key to discovering your needs. This awareness guides you to the books, people and quality experiences that lead toward the development of wholeness and self. It is this wholeness and understanding of self that ignite the fire of intuition. As you nurture this intuition, you will feel yourself becoming much more adept at making the choices in life that are right for your journey. This process is the key to connecting with the bioenvironmental balancing concept. (We will learn more about this concept later in this chapter.)

Another benefit of becoming more intuitive is that you are able to develop a clear and consistent dialogue for speaking to your subconscious mind. Your subconscious mind is the workhorse that cannot be stopped. It labors to carry out every message you send it. Be careful to understand the power of the subconscious mind because it will execute both the positive and negative messages it receives.

The subconscious mind takes "all-comers" and does not discriminate against who, or what, it will serve! That is why it is so important to limit your exposure to negative people and negative situations. We are all faced with hardships that either border on, or are centered in, negative environments. You must be aware of this and - when you have entered such an environment - move to a swift resolution and exit.

You will find that some people or caustic environments

can poison your attitude; this negativity can seep into your character. This point is similar to that made in previous chapters about the power of words. You can't afford negative words to be allowed to permeate your psyche. If so, they will dampen your burning desire to create positive action in your life.

This is because your subconscious mind works all the time, even when you are unaware of it. It's constant functioning is somewhat analogous to breathing. Awake or asleep, you don't need to be reminded or prodded to breathe - it just goes on as a routine aspect of being alive. Similarly, your subconscious mind stays on the job whether you are sleeping or wide-awake. (By the way, at birth you instinctively begin sending messages to the subconscious mind long before you ever utter a single word.)

As you move toward trusting your intuition and becoming bioenvironmentally balanced, your best life becomes a manifestation of your belief system and your thoughts. Thoughts, in other words, create action via the link to the subconscious mind.

You become what you think about most of the time. Why not dramatically help your cause and disposition by feeding positive affirmations and notions to yourself the moment you awaken and just before you go to sleep at night? Functioning in this manner affords you the gift of setting your subconscious mind to run on images of burning desire, hope, faith and triumph! All of these images will place you in a position of feeling good about life and accomplishments. The better you feel, the easier it is for you to leave others feeling good as well.

The JessTalk Life Quadrant Model
- bioenvironmentally balanced lifestyle

It is evident that we do not live in a perfect world and most circumstances are constantly evolving at different rates and present many shades of gray. Your ultimate goal should be to create a world of life-balancing with a lifetime of blissful experiences.

A golden path toward that aim is the Life Quadrant Model. I will explore the components of this model by reviewing the bioenvironmental balancing quest in four distinct quadrants. These four life quadrants hold the absolute principles of bioenvironmental balancing, each representing a best-case scenario of a sustained 25 percent toward total life balancing. Please refer to the illustration below highlighting the quadrants and absolute principles. Note that the heart of this theory rests in the pinnacle of personal power, self-evolution and awakening! (This drawing is similar to the Olympic rings, except that there are four of them interconnecting and the middle contains the term Bioenvironmentally Balanced.)

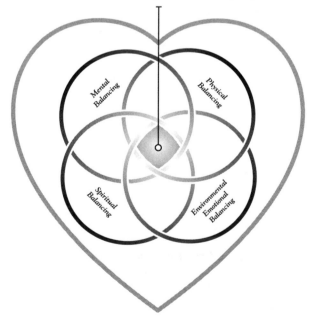

Bioenvironmentally Balanced Lifestyle

Managing the quality of your lifestyle

You must manage the quality of your lifestyle through the power of the Four Life Quadrants. If any one of the life quadrants is out of balance, you will feel out of sorts and you will not function efficiently or effectively. Think of these quadrants as key areas that cover the four fundamental areas that govern your ability to become bioenvironmentally balanced and also act as a measure of your quality of life.

These key areas govern the desired outcome you realize when you fulfill your responsibilities of development; this outcome manifests in a state of biobalancing. The JessTalk Life Quadrant Model, with its key result areas, makes the maximum contribution to yourself, significant others, your lifestyle and the world. The portrayal of the Life Quadrant Model signifies unity. It is this very depiction of solidarity that represents the core operation of growing and developing from the inside out. In other words, this builds harmony from your inner being, while allowing this inner strength to carry over and manifest in the outer world.

JessTalk Life Quadrant Model links affect one another

Each section of the Bioenvironmental Balancing Life Quadrant Model dramatically affects the other. They are interconnected, much like the Olympic rings. If you manage three Life Quadrant areas very well and fail in the fourth quadrant, all other areas will diminish in their capacity to serve you because of the weak link. Better said, your weakest key result area sets the height at which you can develop all your other skills and abilities in the other areas of your Life Quadrant Model.

If you remain unaware of the need to understand the Law of Balance, which of course would suggest you are probably not attending to any of the four sections sufficiently, you will become completely out of balance.

Your inner world can become chaotic. This sets the stage for a train wreck waiting to happen in your outer world! Said another way, to continue in and out of a balanced state of being is equivalent to "dead man walking." You will be asleep at the switch. Do not let yourself spend any time in this area of destructive and disrespectful existence. Change your life by changing your thinking and move from merely existing to actually living a full life. This simple change will always leave you feeling good!

Life Quadrant Model - First Absolute Code Mental Balancing

It should come as no surprise that the First Absolute Code for living a bioenvironmentally balanced lifestyle starts with your mental balancing - your attitude, that is. Your attitude sets the level at which you manifest your potential. A very good way to leave others feeling is to share your positive mental attitude with them, to share your light. Positive energy becomes infectious and people will gravitate to you and want to spend time in your space. You will always leave others feeling good when you have a positive mental attitude.

Further, the Law of Balance says your outer world is a reflection of your inner world. It is prudent to reiterate the axiom "You become what you think about most of the time!" What do you think about most of the time? What are you doing to positively affect your attitude and balancing? Do you spend your free time watching television or reading books? Although watching television probably never killed anyone, there are thousands of studies which note the positive effects that reading has on stimulating the brain. Reading prolongs inner feelings of youth and vivaciousness.

Developing a strong mental attitude - tap into the power of your subconscious mind

Developing a strong mental attitude does not have to be drudgery. Learn to make the learning process fun. Vary your style of learning to keep it interesting. Ask your subconscious mind to bring you the very best teachers in the form of artists, authors, politicians, school kids, grandparents and movies. You can turn a life of learning into one big picture show, starring you as the leading actor. You can make all of your supporting characters life teachers. You can have a great time on your way to enlightenment. How does the thought of starring in your own real-life drama leave you feeling?

Continual learning assists the bioenvironmental balancing process

As you consider the power of enlightenment through the joy of learning, know this: Your perspective and outlook on everything becomes more positive when you embark upon a continual learning program. A great way to launch your continual learning plan is through a dedicated and regimented reading program.

Many studies have proven the positive, rejuvenating effect that a solid reading program has on your mind. This is true regardless of what age you live to be. Pending no disease or disasters, your thought processes remain tuned up and effervescent; life continues to flow. Focusing on this area alone and setting realistic benchmarks for success upholds fully 75 percent of this segment of the life quadrant model. Mental development and balancing are the ultimate markers for setting yourself up for success in managing all life quadrants.

You are bioenvironmentally balanced when your mental, physical, spiritual, emotional and environmental aspects of life are all operating at consistently high levels. That is, they are synergistically and harmoniously working well with one another. A state of bioenvironmental balance affords you the luxury of exponential development on multiple levels.

As you move toward consistently holding the best your life quadrant model has to offer, understand that Mother Nature lends a hand in this process. The assistance nature provides is initiated by your desire to enact the human survival instincts. However, you must keep yourself in optimal health for your survival instincts to kick in and allow Mother Nature to do her job. You cannot afford to allow stress, illness, fatigue, depression, anxiety or any other negative pull to squash your normal mental, physical, spiritual and emotional functioning.

Nature's specific function is to modulate three primal instincts of survival. These are as follows: to eat, to create shelter to avoid being eaten by predators and to have sex for procreation. Dopamine and serotonin are two key neurotransmitters that are responsible for these processes. These two simple amino acids regulate your ability to sustain life. Dopamine is the "go and get it" drug released by the brain; it drives you toward the action needed to maintain life, such as eating or working to provide a livelihood. Serotonin is the drug secreted from the brain that tells us when we have had enough food or work and it signals us to stop. It darkens the landscape so that we can retire from the actions taken to sustain life.

Your attitude adjusts to the level of health sustained in this process of life. Said differently, you must continue to feed your body, mind and soul that which sustains the drive for survival. The healthier you are in managing these basic life needs, the better your general attitude remains. This component of the Life Quadrant Model enables you to persevere toward the other life quadrants, seeking ultimate bioenvironmental balancing.

The connection I would like to point out between the Life Quadrant Model and Mother Nature's assistance is that both are necessary for complete life balancing. This is best viewed as a harmonizing of basic instincts, creative desires and homeostasis. Take a moment to reflect. How does this powerful cocktail of life leave you feeling?

I noted earlier that the need for creating written plans of action in order to internalize your deepest desires should support a call-to-action. The Law of Balance follows that same model of planning. It brings with it unlimited success! This suggests that you must write down your plans for continual mental development.

Life Quadrant Model - Second Absolute Code
Physical Balancing: the gift of stamina invigorates
the life process

The Second Absolute Code of the Life Quadrant Model is that of Physical Balancing. Physical balancing refers to the need your body has for physical fitness. The gift you receive as a result of invoking a good and consistent exercise program is stamina and it serves the life process well. Physical fitness has changed dramatically over the years. In the early days, humans were busy sustaining life by roaming the earth and practicing the art of hunting and gathering.

Humans had a strong exercise program as a result of the desire to find food to sustain the quest for life. Today's Western world is one of convenience and instant gratification. The more conveniently and quickly a product can be consumed, the faster we seem to buy into consumption. In fact, this notion of convenience has made us over-consumers. We no longer get our exercise while hunting for food as in the early days. Now, we must add exercise to our program. In the world of convenience and instant gratification, the notion of exercise escapes many of us.

When you consider designing your exercise program, I recommend starting out with a moderate campaign and building toward a body-stretching and vigorous cardiovascular routine. Vary this program by a weekly strength-training program. Also, I recommend exercising a minimum of one hour per day, three to four days per week. This formula works for nearly anyone, regardless of who you are. Depending on your physical condition, lifestyle and occupation, it could be as much as five to six days per week. Make it part of your lifestyle enhancement program. It should become as natural as breathing. Please consult with your doctor before starting any exercise routine.

In order to truly be successful, choose various forms of exercise that you enjoy. This helps to ensure that you will do them. If walking makes you feel good, walk your way to optimum fitness in nearby parks, around oceans, lakes or beautifully landscaped areas. If basketball suites your fancy, then find yourself a basketball partner ten years your junior and make it your life's mission to teach the young tike a lesson by beating him continually. These suggestions are what I might call living for that rush of adrenaline, which keeps you fit. Dare to embark on the full process; you will not regret it. You will leave yourself feeling good with this life enhancement.

The benefits of a well-planned and consistent exercise program comprise the ingredients that champions are made of. A good program of physical fitness also affects the dopamine and serotonin levels. Dopamine is released in the exercise process and it turns to adrenaline to give you the push to finish a workout. You also get a euphoric feeling after your workout as a result of the chemicals released from the brain that quiet your inner landscape. As a result, you think more clearly and rest better. All of your systems are improved by a good exercise routine.

My lifestyle would not be complete without the blessing of a daily exercise routine. It is simply part of my lifestyle. Some of the benefits include:

1. Mental clarity and focus, being better connected

2. Sustained energy throughout the day

3. Accelerated burning of calories which helps to maintain weight and body symmetry

4. Stronger immune system, resulting in fewer illnesses

5. Staying in tune with my body, vibrancy

6. Stress management

7. Releasing of toxins

I have witnessed countless people turn their lives around by becoming empowered as a result of my supercharged energy. They then created their own power by adding exercise to their lifestyles. In all of the ways mentioned above, my coaching receives an additional boost from this endeavor on the part of clients. Many people understand that they need to follow a good exercise program, but they refuse to do it unless they have a supportive partner to help them stay engaged. I insist that it becomes part of their overall JessTalk Lifestyle Portfolio and personal life plan. They measure their progress by looking for small, yet continual, increases in their physical health via the Law of Accumulation.

Again, the mission is to move through the Life Quadrant Model, creating bioenvironmental balancing. A good physical fitness program aides you in this process. Consider that biobalancing is impossible without the component of physical fitness. Physical balancing gives the gift of stamina, which invigorates the life process.

Life Quadrant Model - Third Absolute Code
Spiritual Balancing: the grounding force

The Third Absolute Code, Spiritual Balancing, is the connection of self with nature's strengths. Spiritual balancing grounds you to the things that are connected in nature so that your being taps into their force. You get the opportunity of being invigorated by using the power of nature, much like receiving what I previously called a two-for-one.

You receive the energy from nature as your spiritual source and it simultaneously becomes linked and integrated with your own life force and personal power. You are as much a part of Mother Nature as the birds and the bees, the flowers and the trees! When you make the unmistakable connection with spirituality and the harmony of nature, your energy levels resonate at higher frequencies. You can't help but be changed for the good through the experience of connecting with the natural world.

Human beings need to listen more closely to the call of nature. We live in a fast-paced society where everyone is jockeying for space and their piece of the planet. Remaining in harmony with the forces of nature sets powers in motion that foster exponential growth in your spiritual balancing. In short, the actual bond between our spiritual longing and the power of nature can be a true revelation.

"Mother nature has a pretty face, but her mood can change in a second."

- Unknown

Remember, however, the laws of nature don't always give us comfort. Sometimes this power manifests itself in overwhelming proportions, which can result in catastrophic events. I have heard it said that Mother Nature has a pretty face, but her mood can change in a second. This can be interpreted to mean: always be vigilant and respectful of the awesome power of nature. Fostering your best aptitude for understanding the connection between self and nature is about coming to terms with the magnitude of that power.

As you strive for balance, the concept of grounding is highly important. It is so important, that you would not be able to sustain any measure of success if you did not have spiritual grounding. All of your efforts would bring fleeting results. You would be missing what I call the "stickiness factor." In other words, spiritual grounding is the glue that holds all other segments of the absolute codes and bioenvironmental balancing processes together. The stickiness factor is key to the definition of spirituality. To maintain spiritual grounding, you must be connected to the forces of nature as you direct your life. Your mental capacity is thus greatly enhanced and everything feels awesome!

Life Quadrant Model - Fourth Absolute Code
Environmental-emotional balancing

The Fourth Absolute Code, Environmental-Emotional Balancing, carries a straightforward meaning and refers to your quest to bring about balance in your emotional state while being subjected to ever-changing environments. This represents a true challenge and suggests that you will have varying states of emotional being. There will be times when you may be low on energy, thus causing you to be low on patience. This would signal an emotional imbalance. Other times you will be fully rested, balanced physically and bursting with fortitude, thus increasing your tolerance levels. This fosters the seeds of an emotionally balanced state of being.

You must be vigilant to disallow negative people or interactions from stealing your energy. Many times the negative situations we find ourselves in aren't personal. It may feel personal because you are on the other end of someone else's diatribe. The truth of the matter is there are a lot of scared and insecure people who may try to attack your character in order to feel better about themselves.

Before you allow yourself to be hurt by people like this, take in the old adage that says, "Consider the source." Keep your reactions positive and proactive. Limit your exposure to people like this because your positive attitude may escalate their attack on your character. Most likely they will have a hard time figuring out what you have to be so cheery about. Negative and insecure types tend to want to maintain their bad moods, rather than be positively influenced by your happy disposition.

Being angry at the world can be a source of energy for negative people. However, manufacturing this type of energy can leave one quite exhausted at the end of the day. This results in a perpetual state of emotional imbalance.

If you find yourself behaving like this, recognize that you are moving into a lower emotional state and take respectful measures toward positive corrections. Some common reasons for perpetuating negative attitudes are:

1. Unrecognized hunger
2. Negative interactions carried over into new situations
3. Emotional immaturity
4. Jealousy or insecurity
5. Poor people skills
6. Anxiety or depression
7. Fear

Recognizing your emotional disposition and adjusting your state accordingly will help increase your emotional balance. Maintaining a level state of emotional balance is a definite way to ensure you are continually leaving others feeling good.

Have you ever considered checking your emotional state of being to see if your behavior is appropriate for certain situations? Can you provide a range of options to serve challenging circumstances?

As you consider what's at stake in not developing these skills, you may reconsider why and how you do things. Firstly, consider why you do the things you do. (The best way to use your energy is to help improve others, self, or circumstances.) Then consider how you do things. Always remember: How you do anything, is how you do everything. Get to the heart of the matter by learning all that you can to improve your understanding and raise the bar on your emotional intelligence.

A positive and strong quality of emotional intelligence will place you in the driver's seat with regard to the Fourth Absolute Code. Your emotional intelligence is the continual maturing of how you respond emotionally. Another benefit for raising the bar on your emotional intelligence is that it will make you a winner in social situations. The crowd pleaser in any situation is that person who is well adjusted and who seems to have the ability to associate with a range of eclectic personality types with ease.

As you become aware and enlightened about your emotional intelligence, the matter of environment must be considered. It is one thing to possess the power of a pleasing personality, winning attitude and a savvy emotional intelligence, but it will mean nothing if you can't moderate its power to fit changing circumstances.

Coming into a situation too cold will send negative messages and may leave your conversationalists feeling as though you are conceited or aloof. Conversely, coming in too hot may falsely broadcast a message of carelessness or lack of respect for others.

I always recommend taking your emotional temperature first. This is followed by a keen reading of the situation. Quickly survey the scene and determine the climate of the conversation and situation before choosing your style of communication. A human barometer reading works well here. Know this: Your sense of measuring people and situations by way of your internal human barometer should fly underneath the radar of others! This reading and measuring process should be seamless and remain undetectable to others. Make your behavior fit the situation and accomplish the desired mission, without compromising integrity and truth. Following these practices presents the best way to adjust emotionally to changing environments.

When you thus exercise the ability to achieve bio-environmental balancing, you demonstrate both your personality and level of awareness. Honing these two sensational qualities is crucial to creating your dreams. The best communicators generally discover ways to use their talents to create awesome lifestyles. They choose their destiny and follow their dreams with the willing support of others. They react to and resolve, demanding situations with satisfaction and grace. They raise their personal effectiveness with these proven techniques and you can do it as well!

Raise your personal effectiveness by bringing your bio-environmental meter to a higher level. Stand by for the incredible connection you will make with others as a result of regularly living this experience. I guarantee that you will leave others wanting more of your time and attention. You will leave them feeling good about themselves and in turn about you as well.

Following the above-mentioned practices is the launching pad for long-term success in the area of becoming bioenvironmentally balanced. The best road to successful, long-term, bioenvironmental balancing is through a daily, weekly, monthly and yearly lifestyle plan that puts you in the driver's seat of your own life. I mentioned the JessTalk Lifestyle Portfolio in the Law of Personal and Professional Development and this component of emotional balance is part of that plan.

If you currently have such a plan, excellent! I applaud your brilliance because you are in a very small group of those who do. If not, consider adopting the suggested JessTalk Lifestyle Bioenvironmental Balancing Plan below. When you closely follow this plan, your life will be on the success path. This path brings about balance and long-term success.

As we close our discussion of the Four Absolute Codes for Living a Bioenvironmentally Balanced Lifestyle and the Life Quadrant Model, be clear on the following key points:

1. The Life Quadrant Model should become your life code for living a complete, balanced existence

2. Becoming bioenvironmentally balanced will make you a giant and continually alter the way in which you attract a life of health and wealth

3. You can't afford not to pay attention to the four quadrants that cover all corners of your life and lead to continual balancing

4. The Life Quadrant Model fully supports the how you leave them feeling concept

5. The best time to start testing this core concept - and enjoying its benefits - is during the reading of this section of the book. If you are like most readers, the "How You Leave Them Feeling" paradigm initially just prompted you make a mental adjustment and commitment to yourself. But now it is time to act on your new mind set and commitment!

Suggested JessTalk Lifestyle Balancing Plan

The Lifestyle Balancing Plan below is within your grasp. With this plan you will be rejuvenated on a daily basis. You will feel happier, lighter and more productive. This program is an excellent way to continually feel great!

1. Morning meditation - Comprises five to fifteen minutes of quiet reflective meditation in order to start your day. This includes giving thanks and appreciation, culminating with creative visualization exercises. Creative visualization consists of closing your eyes and seeing all the quality circumstances, events and people you want to bring into your life. Envision them manifesting before you. It is this vision of how you see yourself living in every aspect of your life that ensures that it becomes your reality.

2. Spend two to five minutes reading affirmations - Make sure your affirmations cover the full spectrum of the life you want to live. Keep continual growth and development at the top of your affirmation list, regardless of your level of success.

3. Spend two to five minutes reading your motives list - Your motives list is a list of benefits associated with your goals and aspirations. This list represents your motivation (motives) for why you are committed to honoring the promises you have made to yourself. Understanding the full benefits of your motives is stimulating and allows clear reasoning for actions taken.

4. Fifteen minutes to one hour of physical fitness daily - This includes walking and aerobic exercise, accompanied by strength training and conditioning. Pick an activity that you love doing; this will ensure that you stay on your program. Add at least one cross-training activity that involves muscles you

do not use during your primary exercise program. Pick a reliable partner and set fitness, weight, body fat, body symmetry and healthy eating goals. Challenge one another to move toward continual improvement. Before you reach your goals, set new benchmarks of success and measure your results.

5. Embark on your normal routine of life - Approach responsibilities with fresh vigor gained from your morning meditation program and visualization exercises. See things as you are, not as they are!

6. Healthy eating regimen - Choose an eating program that is right for your metabolism and body type. Make sure it is a program that you can remain committed to for life. Please don't push yourself into fad diets that can often leave you in a worse position than when you began. After selecting the right plan for yourself, commit to a "5:2" schedule, that is, five days on your program and two days where you might enjoy the foods you like. There will be some cases where a 6:1 ratio is necessary to gain the life balance you are looking for.

7. Other sources of influence - Some additional sources and activities include: reading, movies, friends, clients, family, decompression day, "pamper-me" week, weekend retreats, doctor's visits and so on.

Stress Management 101

As I discuss lifestyle balancing, I must speak to a very common phenomenon that people face on a daily basis: stress. Humans are routinely exposed to numerous forms of stress throughout life. It is inescapable. The best way to deal with stress is to manage the types of stress that can be resolved and relieve yourself of the stress that is out of your control. If this sounds like Stress Management 101, you are right, because it is. Returning to basics is the key to long-term stress management relief.

Although there are countless ways to deal with the various types of stress, the solution lies in three main strategies. The first is the measurement of the type of stress and what impact it has made on persons and circumstances. The second main strategy involves dismantling a stressful situation by determining the easiest way to resolution. Finally, the third primary strategy is to determine the best way to create and to maintain an environment of manageable stress.

Some folks say that admitting that they are stressed out makes them feel like they are portraying weakness. Many people, especially men, will not seek the help they need. This is unfortunate, for incurring stress is not a sign of weakness. In fact, it is a very human and normal experience.

Today's world resonates with various kinds of stress. We might face anything from the continued anomalies in our weather patterns, to grieving a loss, to incurring stressful debt. This short list highlights some of the more commonplace stresses of contemporary life:

1. Environmental stress
2. Corporate stress
3. Family stress
4. Relationship stress
5. Mental stress
6. Physical stress
7. Social stress
8. Post-traumatic stress
9. Life stress
10. Financial stress
11. Debtor stress

Each form of stress needs different tactics for resolution. Regardless of its type, stress can take its toll on your mental, physical, spiritual and emotional balancing. In the face of stress, you must find outlets and management systems that reduce or eradicate the stress in order to maintain proper balance.

Key Action Steps
The Law of Balance

Action Step 1
Learn to control your life and destiny

You are responsible for your own life. Regardless of where you are now, take the time to evaluate whether you are on course for the life you desire and deserve. Take control by either developing or improving your lifestyle portfolio. This single step alone ensures that you create your own destiny.

Action Step 2
Practice the Four Absolute Codes for balance

Use the power of the Absolute Codes for living a bio-environmentally balanced lifestyle. This increases your quality of life. Embark on a reading program to stimulate your mental balancing. Create a model for exercising. Learn to connect with nature to facilitate spiritual and environmental-emotional balancing.

Action Step 3
Use the interconnections of the Life Quadrant Model

Pay close attention to the Four Absolute Codes mentioned above. Monitoring the balance of these codes helps alert you to breaches in any of your major result areas. The best time to boost your energy and attention in areas of your Life Quadrant is at the beginning of a slump. Take swift action to increase the intensity for all areas of the Life Quadrant. This is in order to avoid any one area depleting all of the other higher-performing result areas. The best bioenvironmentally state of being resonates at higher levels as a direct result of early detection of trouble.

Action Step 4
Manage negative stress

People are routinely exposed to numerous forms of negative stress in daily life. Determine whether you are
being subjected to negative stress. If you find yourself
subjected to various forms of negative stress, isolate the
root of the stress and design an immediate plan for
releasing it. Always keep the end result in mind when
working on relieving yourself of stressful situations and
elect the solution with the least amount of resistance.

Action Step 5
Follow a healthy lifestyle plan

Good health is the precursor for all that is good to
follow. Review the suggested JessTalk Lifestyle Balancing Plan for maintaining your health. Make this plan
an integral part of your lifestyle, rather than something
extra that you might not sufficiently prioritize.

Summary Points
The Seventh Essential Law of Life
The Law of Balance

1. There is nothing more powerful than knowing that you have full control over your life and destiny

2. The key to living a balanced life is in understanding the full paradigm of balance and each of its major components

3. A bioenvironmentally balanced lifestyle is born of the Four Absolute Codes

4. Mental, physical, spiritual and environmental -emotional balancing are at the root of the Four Absolute Codes in the JessTalk Life Quadrant Model

5. Stress Management 101 is a return to the basics of life

Affirmations
Moments for Reflection

1. I take responsibility for my own happiness and my life journey

2. I am bioenvironmentally balanced as a result of my choices and discipline

3. My level of intensity remains high as I follow the Life Quadrant Model

4. I do not allow negative stress to become part of my world

5. I enjoy my healthy lifestyle plan and receive maximum benefits from it

A World of Appreciation

The dream of this book was conceived during a special coaching session I was conducting with one of the CEO's of my JessTalk Coaching Lifestyles Program. This was a special session of conflict resolution. I was trying to get the CEO to understand a point regarding how he could handle a conflict with one of his employees.

After several attempts at trying to get him to empathize with the conditions of the situation, it was clear to me that I was not going to get him to understand my point. I offered this as my final closing point: "I understand what it is you are looking for from your employee and he probably understands it as well. Yet if you truly want to get the results you are espousing, then at the end of the day, it's about how you leave him feeling!"

Following that session, I couldn't stop thinking about how many things the one phrase, how you leave them feeling, meant - both in the session and in life in general. The full understanding and application of the concept amount to a complete strategy for helping others get what they want and need - and for getting what you want and need. This has profound implications. The concept how you leave them feeling offers the answers to how you get things done! In this way, it is your ultimate key to personal and professional success.

I spent the next twenty-four hours consumed with thoughts of how many people could be helped with the understanding of this one simple message. I began writing notes of all the benefits one could receive by adhering to the theory of how you leave them feeling. I emerged from this fury of brainstorming and realized that I had been living this theory for as long as I could remember. Thus far, I had never felt the need to find words for this uniquely simple way of approaching life.

Due to my quest to help as many people as I can, I thought: "What better way to help legions of people than to give them the simple, yet effective tools for discovering answers to one of life's most illusive areas?" I also thought: "How do I live a life of happiness and fulfillment? How did I learn how to navigate through the minefields of life and find a harmonious balance of serving others as I serve myself?" How You Leave Them Feeling offers other people those answers. The concepts in this book are so simple that one can start improving, and obtain meaningful, measurable results immediately. You don't need multiple college degrees or years of psychology in order to reap the benefits of the how you leave them feeling ideology.

I have had countless teachers along my success journey and I remain appreciative of them all. As noted throughout the writing of this book, I have demonstrated my love and respect for those who reside in my global village. But there have been teachers whom I have encountered who delivered harsh life lessons with hardened hearts. Despite the pain they caused me and others in enduring their tough lessons, I thank them as well. All that I have learned, even from the most unsympathetic of teachers, is a lifeline to all that I am today.

I must offer special thanks to the close circle of second-family members, friends and colleagues who I call my "content readers." Appreciation goes to: Robert Ciccone, Christina Ciccone, Bruce Davis, Ann Lee, Daryl Odom, Cher Weldon and Eric Zilewicz. You helped critique "How You Leave Them Feeling" and your validation was very important to me and to the writing of this book. I realize that all of you live very busy lives, managing household responsibilities and running major companies. I have heard it said that "If you really want to get something done, give it to a busy person." This project would have had a quite different outcome to it without your expertise and input. Thank you!

I have a world of appreciation for the quality of life I have been able to create thus far. I know that I'm in the infancy stages of my development and the light shines brightly. I continue to live in the present while planning for those portions of my future that lend themselves to forethought. I trust and appreciate that all else will arrive as a result of the karma I create.

My spirit is constantly being refreshed. This gives me strength, while restoring my intuition. With all my heart, I thank God for entrusting me with the message of "How You Leave Them Feeling". I'm happy to carry the torch of sharing this message with those who continually strive to improve their quality of life.

I respect and cherish the seven essential laws profiled in this book. I encourage you to explore these laws and use them to live the life you deserve. I use these laws for myself, family members, friends, colleagues and strangers. The best use of these laws has served me well! I refuse to imagine what kind of life I might have had without the understanding and use of these laws. I extend my warmest regard to the global village and my second-family relationships. I enjoy the notion that the village is still shining the light!

I appreciate that you have taken the time to read this book. I trust that you have gained positive and useful information as a trade-off for your time spent. If you are able to change one life with the information found in this book, then the hundreds of hours that have gone into accumulating the concepts and writing the text have been worth it. If you count on one thing alone to make a positive difference in your life, and in the lives of others, feel secure in knowing that the power of how you leave them feeling will always make you a winner.

About the Author

Jesse Ferrell's work represents a celebration of life and a mastery of the quest for living a life of abundance. His message about using the seven essential laws of life is evident in his powerful keynote addresses, workshops and leadership development seminars. The JessTalk Coaching Lifestyles Program offers continued and systematic approaches that challenge clients to live the life they deserve by observing the daily practice of how you leave them feeling. His mission is to help others experience the everyday epiphanies that light the road to ultimate abundance and success.

Jesse Ferrell is the founder, President and CEO of JessTalk Speaking Services LLC, headquartered in Las Vegas, Nevada. His company has numerous domestic and international affiliations. He lives in Las Vegas, Nevada, with his wife Teresa and loyal companion Casey, a 22-pound golden retriever.

Jesse Ferrell would like to hear from you if you are interested in receiving the How You Leave Them Feeling newsletter, JessTalk Speaks newsletter and future books by the author. You can find other helpful information on his websites. Please go to the following websites for additional information:

www.howyouleavethemfeeling.com

www.jesstalk.com

How You Leave Them Feeling
8550 West Charleston Blvd. Suite #102-166
Las Vegas, Nevada 89117

Jesse Ferrell maintains a full schedule of JessTalk Coaching Lifestyle clients, but he is always open to inquiries. He is also available for Corporate Team Coaching programs, lectures, workshops and seminars. All details from inquiries will be sent upon request.

Recommended Reading

"How to Become a Debt Free Millionaire"
Boaz & Greta Rauchwerger

"Goals!"
Brian Tracy

"The Psychology of Success"
Brian Tracy

"Action Strategies for Personal Achievement"
Brian Tracy

"Thinking Big"
Brian Tracy

"21 Secrets of Self Made Millionaires"
Brian Tracy

"Time Power - A Proven System for Getting More Done In Less Time
Than You Ever Thought Possible"
Brian Tracy

"Change Your Thinking Change Your Life"
Brian Tracy

"Take Time for Your Life"
Cheryl Richardson

"Samurai Selling"
Chuck Laughlin/Karen Sage

"The Magic of Believing"
Claude M. Bristol

"Playing For Keeps - Michael Jordan"
David Halberstam

"Winning Ways 4 Secrets for Getting Great Results by Working Well
With People"
Dick Lyles

"The Four Agreements"
Don Miguel Ruiz

"The Power of Your Subconscious Mind"
Dr. Joseph Murphy

"The Craving Brain"
Dr. Ronald Ruden

"The Power of Intention"
Dr. Wayne W. Dyer

"The Richest Man in Babylon"
George S. Clason

"The Disease to Please"
Harriet B. Braiker Ph.D.

"Jung: Interpreting Your Dreams"
James A. Hall M.D.

"The Celestine Prophecy"
James Redfield

"Getting Everything You Can Out of All You've Got"
Jay Abraham

"Take Charge of Your Life"
Jim Rohn

"More Than a Pink Cadillac"
Jim Underwood

"The Winner in You - Be Your Own Hero"
Joe Gilliam

"Healing the Shame that Binds You"
John Bradshaw

"Bradshaw on the Family"
John Bradshaw

"21 Minutes in a Leader's Day"
John C. Maxwell

"Your Road Map For Success"
John C. Maxwell

"Failing Forward"
John C. Maxwell

"The 17 Essential Qualities of a Team Player"
John C. Maxwell

"The Laws of Inner Wealth"
John Templeton

"Don't Know Much About the Bible"
Kenneth C. Davis

"Bird Watching"
Larry Bird with Jackie MacMull

"Live Your Dreams"
Les Brown

"Blink"
Malcolm Gladwell

"The Tipping Point"
Malcolm Gladwell

"The Instant Millionaire"
Mark Fisher

"Miracles Happen"
Mary Kay Ash

"Codependent's Guide to the 12 Steps"
Melody Beattie

"Think & Grow Rich"
Napoleon Hill

"The Power of Positive Thinking"
Norman Vincent Peale

"The Autobiography of Quincy Jones"
Quincy Jones

"Coping with Difficult People"
Robert Blamson

"Retire Young Retire Rich"
Robert T. Kiyosaki

"The Cash Flow Quadrant"
Robert T. Kiyosaki

"Rich Dad's Guide to Investing"
Robert T. Kiyosaki

"Rich Dad Poor Dad"
Robert T. Kiyosaki

"Me & Hank: A Boy & His Hero, 25 Years Later"
Sandy Tolan

"The Measure of a Man: A Spiritual Biography"
Sidney Poitier

"Who Moved My Cheese"
Spencer Johnson M.D.

"You Can Make it Happen - A 9 Step Plan for Success"
Stedman Graham

"What Do I Say Next? Talking Your Way to Business & Social Success"
Susan Roane

"The 9 Steps to Financial Freedom"
Suze Orman

"The Laws of Money, The Lessons of Life"
Suze Orman

"The Road to Wealth"
Suze Orman

"Money Wisdom"
Suze Orman

"The Courage to be Rich"
Suze Orman

"Tiger Woods - The Making of a Champion"
Tim Rosaforte